THE ART OF
NILNESS

Where Mind and Reality Converge

ANIL KANTHI

For permissions or further information, please contact:
Email: anilkanthi@gmail.com

Dedication.

I dedicate this book to my mother Shakuntala—**Awwa**, who did not let life's difficulties corrupt the unconditional love she has always given me; to my father Vitthal—**Appa,** who grounded me with simplicity; and to my partner—**Dilmi**, who lit me with her pure love, uprooted all my turmoils, accepted me for who I am, and turned me into gold from the ore I was.

Preface.

The paradox of life is that one cannot see the depths of life without suffering. None of us want to choose to suffer, but it is inevitable, and those who have suffered somehow have the prerequisite to work toward living life deeply. The writings here are not to change the world but to shift the perspective of the reader from the illusions of the mind to living in reality.

I started writing the contents of this book in February 2023, and it was only towards the end of 2024 that I thought of turning thousands of notes into a book that you read now with ten chapters and 88 timeless lessons. I wrote **The Art of Nilness** to spread awareness of reality and let others know that there is an entirely deep way of living life that lies beyond mere words and the creations of the mind. You and I are one of the creations in this physical world that we experience on a daily basis, and this daily life has become a norm for most of us. But, to experience life with depth is a completely different ball game altogether. It is here where the magic of life lies.

The Art of Nilness gives an insight into how we are as humans today and what it takes to perceive the truth. The truth that many wish to find out but only end up talking about with their self-held beliefs, understanding, and experiences.

Truth or reality cannot be experienced or spoken about. It is beyond human speech, experience, senses, emotions, logic, imagination, and mortality. Everything around the truth can be described. But trying to put the truth itself into words is futile as the truth is indescribable_and beyond the commonly held notions of comprehension.

If understanding was the way to realize the truth, the abundant knowledge that is there today in the year 2024 should have made everybody who is socially intelligent enough enlightened. But that is not the case because knowledge only has its place to keep moving humanity forward in terms of progress and evolution as a species.

It's the mind that is designed innately to grasp and hold on to what it creates psychologically. As each human who is born into this world comes with the mind, though it feels like a herculean task to find the truth, all that a person needs to have are the qualities of simplicity, courage, attention, observation, and ending.

None of these are different from the other. Though the words may have different meanings, that which is being pointed at through words is the real thing. It is an essence of what we experience and deeply perceive. But the world we are in now has very few people who would actually want to look at anything the words themselves point to, as they are content with the words, the meanings they derive, and the sense they make out of the words throughout their lives.

In this book, I explore the subtleties of reality. The subtleties that are waiting to be found—can only be found when an individual has the yearning to know the depths of what this life is all about. Am I here just to live and die one day, suffering all the way to death? Or is there something I can dive into that would enrich the quality of my life and give it that spark that never goes away?

That purpose beyond the meanings and interpretations. That meaning in front of which the words fall flat. That seeing where there is no you and me but only the oneness of reality where the mind is never a problem. The mind is not an enemy.

For everybody to understand, **The Art of Nilness** has simplicity and day-to-day life at the heart of its writings, making it a valuable investment of time, as the return is not only manifold but priceless for its insightful & transformative capabilities over the course of one's lifetime. I say this with confidence as the real-life applications of **The Art of Nilness** transformed my own life. Even though I was living it, it is only now that I can speak about it verbally to put forth to the world. I hope it becomes a launchpad to transform your life, too.

In all, **The Art of Nilness** conveys spirituality in a way that is rarely available—straightforward without unnecessary complications, practical and direct, without any bias or personal agenda, and in a way where readers can directly perceive reality without the interference of the constructs of the mind.

Before you begin with the book, You and I need to meet at a place that is aligned at the root. Only then can two people dive into deeper matters that are of colossal significance to the quality of our lives.

+ Read as if you know nothing.

+ Read as if you are reading for the very first time.

+ Do not worry—the memories are not going anywhere, but if you can put them aside while you start reading this book—there is a possibility for a deeper perspective to seep into your being, which only knows one direction—*deeper*.

What this book is not about:

+   There is no quick fix to understanding and introspection. It takes time and effort. If one is not looking for a long-term solution to all the problems they currently face, I would politely ask you to put this book down as this is *not* a book for short-term gratification. This is for people who seek depth in life. Who *wants* depth in life.

+   **Nilness** in itself has no meaning whatsoever. It is void of any and all human activities, be it physical or psychological. But **Nilness** *doesn't* imply nothingness or emptiness. Rather, **Nilness** represents a state of pure potential, a void where all possibilities exist. It's being beyond the limitations of the physical world, where you become free of the constraints of the mind.

+   This is not a book to achieve something. It is a book that is devoid of reaching a destination but with an arrival that has no start or end.

+   Unlike many books, the content of **The Art of Nilness** was not driven by sales. The book was *not* written with selling as an intention. The contents of **The Art of Nilness** were written consciously over a period of two years & created purely with the sole purpose of imparting depth.

+   I do not provide any system to be followed, as the mind functions with a series of interconnected systems in place. Anything the mind can use to create a new set of systems or patterns is carefully excluded from the book. In fact the book is written intentionally to avoid systematisation.

What this book is about:

+   The limitation of being a human is that one can only express through our created words and with the biases of human perceptible experiences. The way I go about showing what is intangible is by throwing light on all that is hindering a human being from looking at reality.

+ All the topics are written in a way that showers light on all that is blocking out the truth in an unconscious mind.

+ **The Art of Nilness** is for those who have the patience or wish to develop the patience to look at their own life to see the world for what it is in actuality and not for what they want to think it is, to be consoled with false reality.

+ Although the book is written for everybody, those who will gain the most out of it and connect with the contents instantly are those who are patient, sensitive, observant, have simplicity in their heart, introverts, open-minded, serious, problem-solvers, innovative, imaginative, perceptive, reflective contemplative, zealous, compassionate, humble, kind, intuitive, inquisitive, writers, readers, curious, resilient, antifragile, empathetic, and calm.
If you have any of these traits—Welcome Home.
If you don't have any of these traits—Come Ashore.

+ If one is ready to receive, come ashore to leave the storms of the mind behind and *begin a life with awareness & depth.*

~

Table of Contents

Chapter IV — Human Relationships.

Chapter V — Insight of You.

Chapter VI — The Art of Eliminating.

Chapter VII — Beyond Humanity.

Chapter VIII — The Art of Sensitivity.

Introduction.

Right at the beginning, I will make one thing clear. What I share is words but the words do not have any significance. What one needs to emphasize is the context and the view in which the words are used for.

Do not get attached to the words, for they themselves have the potency to become a barrier.

Do not derive meanings or validations out of it as to whether it is wrong or it is right. There is no right or wrong in reality, as these are creations of the human mind. Among human behavior, there are rights or wrongdoings, but in reality, there is nothing as such.

Read, reflect, and reap the benefits of what you connect with and feel the need to grow in as an individual who has to survive, prosper, and live in the world created by fellow humans.

The ultimate reaping happens when one reads, keeping all their baggage aside and looks at what is conveyed freshly as if you have just begun to finally work out what it is all about.

Reading with such a mindset where you are anew, where you trust what is being said, knowing it is coming from a genuine source, and imbibing it with questioning and reflecting on all that you have ever known, understood, and experienced will put you in a position and the power to view from a distance and closeness at the same time.

The words that will be used may sound contradictory when used for a different conveying but the context of when they are used is what matters the most. The most ideal way of going about the writing is to read deliberately, soak in the information, understand the words for what they are, and see the reality for yourself.

People who will benefit the most from what I express are those who have a strong urge to overcome the limitations that they know they do have and are on the verge of eliminating them but are either afraid or do not know how to or what is on the other side.

The book is equivalent to clarity over a lot of things that are not easily available or spoken about in a way that people can first understand, then experience on their own and implement them in their lives to witness a drastic change in the quality and depth of everyday life.

Each human born into the world comes with an innate ability to live consciously, but the unconscious world around him or her shapes their mind to what already exists in their environment. Later on, it becomes the responsibility of the individual to see that they were conditioned all this while and then work their way out of it—to have complete freedom from the environment and the world in order to start living life in a new way that has depth and awareness of everything.

~

CHAPTER I — CURRENT HUMAN CONDITION.

We named ourselves human beings. No other species or entity calls us that.

Labeling something is for recognition only. But if we become identified with the words we use to recognize and differentiate one from the other, there will be a lack of oneness in an individual's experience, which is quite evident if you look at the world around us.

The word *world* is not the world itself. One cannot actually see the entire world at once. When you read the word *world*, there is an image in the mind that comes about since you already have a thousand meanings assigned to it based on your experiences. The same is the case with all the words of the English language and all the languages of the human world.

You cannot truly experience the unfiltered reality as it is when there is so much significance given to the very words that are used by the mind that, in turn, shapes the views you have, how you see things, and what meanings you end up deriving out of people and life.

As I write this in 2024, it saddens me to see the state of what we as human species have become. Divisions created by the mind have spread so far and deep that the separative way of being has become the foundation of living for most people.

This is why each one of us suffers.

There are actual problems to deal with in life, but then there are problems that one goes on creating within oneself that arise out of living in the contents and activities of the mind.

The problems that exist in the world were created by the mind. The solution cannot come out of it.

This is why it is most important to be open about the possibility that there is a way to live that is not amidst what the mind creates.

The human condition that we find ourselves in today cannot be solved all at once but one person at a time. There is no pressing a button to eradicate all problems at once. It is a long ordeal that you and I, as the responsible ones in this beautiful human experience, need to partake in voluntarily.

+ You want to change the world.

+ To do that, you need to contribute to it.

+ In order to do that, you need to first understand the current situation of the world.

+ To do this, you must be able to *observe* what the world is and all the things that are happening—without any interpretation.

+ And then, with sheer awareness, one can first realize the truth and go about telling others that it is indeed a possibility.

+ This is the only way one can truly change the world.

Lesson 1 — People Are Unique.

Stop thinking in the direction that the world or a person is weird or bad or toxic or disturbed or unstable and all the other labels that the mind has clung to. Put a halt to continuing the automated overflow of thoughts that the mind is used to.

People are unique because
They have had their own life experiences.
Each human is different from the other.
No two people can have the same interpretation.
Each person has their own principles, ideologies, beliefs, ego, philosophy, approach, understanding, opinions, patterns, learning, dreams, desires, personality, attachments, regrets, goals, perspectives, emotions, values, behavior, thinking, and way of living.

You choose the people in your life.
It is you who allows the people to be in your life.
It is you who rents out a significant amount of space in the mind for those people.

If you are someone who wants to move in a better direction, live in a peaceful way, and have a free yet practical lifestyle—all you need to do is to evict the space you continuously rent out in the mind to everything that is compulsive.

It is simple. This takes a degree of awareness to start cultivating such an application to become free of the contents of the mind. The process of eviction, ironically, has everything to do with *you* and not other people or all that the mind thinks and imagines about.

If we start observing and get to a point of creating order out of the chaos, that is when the real shift starts to occur. It begins to happen because the mind, by its nature, moves towards making sense and creating order out of what it has experienced.

But the problem is that most people's mind (not minds, but

mind-singular) have become accustomed to creating disorder out of order as the negative experiences are predominant. The mind takes that and wraps it up with the basic necessities for survival, be it physically or mentally. These become the identity and personality of a person at the foundational level.

As this is being done over and over and over again, the negative experiences re-emphasize to the person that this is the only way to protect myself and go about in life. Such people's compulsive mind operate with fear as the main factor; it is only going to create more chaos and not order. Unfortunately, as most people function in such a way, the world at large is in disarray.

Now, taking all of this into consideration, along with the fact that our mind moves towards what we focus on in the present, taking with it all of its content throughout an individual's lifespan, it is quite obvious it is a distorted view.

Consider what is seen directly through our naked eyes. If one sees through a filter that is placed in front of the eyes, the sight changes according to the filter that is in between the eyes and the view. Adding layers of filters changes how the view is experienced and blocks out the actual view. With the filter of the activities of the mind, a person only ends up creating more and more disorder instead of creating order from chaos.

Just as the other person is unique and has their own characteristics—*you*, my friend, have your own principles, ideologies, beliefs, ego, philosophy, approach, understanding, opinions, patterns, learning, dreams, desires, personality, attachments, regrets, goals, perspectives, emotions, values, behavior, thinking, and way of living.

You, too, have what the rest of humanity has.

Sink that in for a bit. Read it again and ponder.

Unless we start questioning every single aspect of what it means to exist as a human, the depth of humanity will always be amiss.

~

Lesson 2 — There is no Best in Reality.

Everyone wants to be the best in whatever they are doing, or at least they boast they are the best in some way or the other.

Best insurance. Best car.
Best book. Best apartment.
Best restaurant. Best hotel.
Best country. Best company.
Best government. Best movie.
Best person. Best god.
Best school. Best university.
Best product. Best service.
Best hospital. Best airport.
Best clothes. Best doctor.
Best teacher. Best work.
Best plant. Best animal.
Best couple. Best parents.
Best family. Best child.
Best house. Best life.

This luring to instill comparison in the mind of others is how people like you and me learn to start placing something or someone else at a high standard in the first place.

The problem here is that *the best* keeps changing on the outside as per the necessities of society and people. But if the person who learned it ends up sticking to that belief and does not see that the ever-changing outside was not an ideal source of learning to begin with, that will keep the person stagnant, always falling prey to the direction in which the society moves taking a huge mass of people along with it.

Do not fall prey to the tactics of an ever-changing world. You will have no ground to base yourself on if you do.

We have to stop, question, and take matters into our own hands to see that there is nothing best by itself. The outcomes of human endeavor will always be comparative, but there is no need for comparison when it comes to psychological activities, no matter what it is.

Comparison happens between the two. It cannot happen with just one. This is the mind dividing what passes through it into myriads of separation.

Reality comes alive when the mind stops to filter the happenings and stops obstructing its view. The thing about the mind is that it is never going to stop functioning, no matter who the human is. The mind can stop obscuring the view of reality only and only when we deeply observe everything as it is. Your partner, your thoughts, the words that other people speak, their behavior, the bird, the tree, the cloud, all of it must be seen without the contents of the mind being involved in that seeing.

Then, you will see that there is not a single thing in existence that is better than another. Each and everything has beauty in it. The society has bestified everything so that it can be looked at and followed by the majority. The majority will follow as they want another person to show them the way, to lead the pack. This is an addiction to being told what to do, how to be, what not to do—a clear cut defined way to live.

Do you see the danger of following such a system? The mind itself needs a system to thrive on but the reality is void of any such things.

Are you a person who wants to follow another person and society to live as it has been decided by their compulsive mind?

Or are you a person who wants to be free of all the limitations of life in order to clearly see the oneness of reality as it is, where the mind is never a problem anymore?

~

Lesson 3 — The Illusion of Innovation.

We have been hoodwinked by our own mind. Every innovation, every word we have coined, is rooted in reality itself. Take cloud storage, for instance—inspired by the very clouds above us, vast, moveable, and omnipresent, yet never touching the ground.

The business of manipulation:

In the corporate arena, words are not just tools for communication. They are mechanisms of manipulation. They tap into the psyche, subtly guiding the unfocused mind of the masses. Here, the elite people of our time have mastered the art of psychological influence, steering humanity in directions where 99.99% are oblivious to the puppetry at play. This is why followers outnumber leaders by far, creating a world where the unconscious majority seeks guidance from the few, fostering inequality.

The mirror of technology:

Artificial Intelligence, Machine Learning—these aren't just technological advancements. They are reflections of our own mental processes. The technological world has taken the essence of how the brain works and turned it into algorithms and robotics, enhancing our lives. Yet, what often goes unnoticed is how these technologies exploit the same human fascination with novelty that we have always had, pulling us in with the allure of new information and gadgets.

Awakening to the copycat nature:

Once you realize that all human creation is merely mimicking the external world and our internal experiences, the charm of the modern, materialistic world begins to fade. This realization is profound. It is not just understanding with the mind but a deep, transformative awareness.

+ Consciousness Unveiled: When an individual awakens to this truth, there is no going back. This consciousness starts to infiltrate every unconscious action, thought, and belief.

+ The Spread of Awareness: Like a seed planted in fertile ground, this awareness grows, spreading through the unconscious layers of one's psyche, unstoppable once it begins.

This journey into self-realization reveals that the creator and the creation are not separate—they are one and whole. It is an insight that transcends mere intellectual comprehension, touching the very essence of existence.

In recognizing that our innovations are but reflections of nature and our inner selves, we unlock a powerful potential to not just consume but to truly comprehend and evolve.

~

Lesson 4 — The World Needs Originality.

The world doesn't need something that is already there.

The world doesn't need the next Charles Darwin.
The world doesn't need the next Albert Einstein.
The world doesn't need the next Mahatma Gandhi.
The world doesn't need the next Steve Jobs.
The world doesn't need the next J K Rowling.
The world doesn't need the next Satoshi Nakamoto.
The world doesn't need the next Warren Buffet.
The world doesn't need the next Barack Obama.
The world doesn't need the next Bill Gates.
The world doesn't need the next Elon Musk.

There are thousands of people who have changed the world with their life's work. They do inspire us immensely. However, if one spends their entire life trying to be the next so and so, that itself is a recipe for disaster even if they end up being that next.

It's so easy to lose originality with all the information we get bombarded with in our modern world. We live in a time unlike ever before, where there are mountains of data out there about things that already exist, about the accomplishments we human beings have already achieved. This was not possible to have in the comfort of our living rooms until the 21st century.

Growth can either be on top of the already existing domains or out of something entirely different altogether. The latter would do justice to the growth of us as a species for the remainder of the 21st century because recycling what has been there is not an actual invention or a discovery in its truest form.

For example, every year, a new iPhone is launched with new features. It's the progress in technology that makes it the world's number-one company. But the base of it remains the same although new products are launched. And this is true for all the companies out there. The point is, yes—we need these for our own convenience in various ways. But we also need original thinking, which would lead to the discovery of dimensions we haven't yet gotten a grasp of.

What the world needs more of is an expression of individuals in their own pristine form—not built on top of the past but created out of curiosity of the unknown.

All the people who have created something that seemed impossible or weird at that time had one thing in common—their own originality.

They didn't let the world suppress their true nature or their way of thinking. Sure, the times they lived in had an impact on how much they could express themselves, but that didn't let them bog down and follow the herd. They stood out of the crowd and took the other direction to pave their own future, no matter how different it looked in the eyes of other people.

The world needs inspiration.
The world needs a new generation of original thinkers in all domains.
The world needs visionaries whose very way of living creates a humbling ripple effect for generations to come.

Above all, the world needs people who are as selfless as possible and do what's needed for the betterment of humanity & the world.

The world needs the next *you.*

The world needs *originality.*

~

Lesson 5 — True Originality.

How we see others doing their work in the direction of what we ourselves are aiming to do, in itself, becomes a limitation due to the copying mechanism of the mind.

Misled persuasion:

What we see over the internet has a lot of subtle influences that tend to permeate into the mind, sometimes irrevocably.
Marketing has destroyed the usage of words and corrupted them with the intention to sell. All of the marketing that we see today has exploited and wrongly used human psychology to influence and persuade the masses of people who do not understand psychology to buy.

True originality is in knowing that other people are doing such an activity and being free from it to allow yourself to do it in your own way with your own perception and originality.

The mind categorizes. All of our studies, research, trying to make others understand a topic, or anything that is split into categories or lists is all *aiding* the mind in deepening the very way it functions.

Because the mind works in this way, you can see that the entire human world is categorized.

Sink that in.

The mind cannot be seen for what it is when you are inside its categorized contents. There is no information in that content that is of significance to this unending moment, which is all there is, all there ever was, and all there ever will be.

~

Lesson 6 — Like, Share, Obsess: The Digital Craze for Validation.

Our deep psychological needs are turned into digital obsessions.

The world has taken our psychological needs and turned them into an obsession, knowing very well those are the deep, unfulfilled emotional needs that each of us has in some way or the other.

+ The like button mirrors our real-life need to be liked by another person.

+ A job portal mirrors our need to work for our survival in real life.

+ The emoticons and gifs mirror what we feel and identify with in real life.

+ Requests from a stranger to connect online mirror the real-life need to be with a person.

Humankind's most straightforward needs have been removed from real life and mirrored in a virtual world. If one doesn't see this, one gets hooked on the needs fulfilled online but fundamentally lacking in real life.

Why is it so difficult to observe all the manipulations the unconscious world performs in the name of human evolution? Yes, we benefit significantly from these inventions, but there are more cons than pros.

The ultimate loss is that a person loses touch with reality, which is challenging to figure out due to the complexity of the mind. How can one see what the mind is in reality when one's needs are being fulfilled virtually? They wouldn't even bother to examine their way of existing and daily living, as the momentum in the virtual world is too strong to let go of.

It is strong because the mind holds information dear, and it is impossible to see the mind with all its activities when a person is involved in its contents. The internet contains ridiculously intense content that the mind can repeatedly access.

The problem of not seeing the mind, reality, or the truth for what it is has existed for ages. But with today's technologies, *simply seeing* is becoming increasingly difficult.

+ To simply look at our own lives.

+ To observe.

+ To pay attention to ourselves.

+ To simply be.

~

Lesson 7 — God is an Idea.

Anything that exists out of the memory or information **of** the mind is still the content of the mind.

The mind has ways to keep its illusions alive through its information, knowledge, content, or call it anything. The mind has its own place, but it has no place if one wants to observe what the truth or the reality is or what the mind itself is.

The question "Who is observing the mind?" still is a question that keeps the basis that there are *two*. That there is a division already, that *something* is observing the mind.

This happens because of our conditioning in childhood to *always* look at things as *this is mine* and *that is not mine*. That *this is you* and *that is not you*. Such fundamental conditionings go deep into our very perception.

It is hard to use words, as it is still information, to convey what is conceptualised as God.
The true God is not a creation of the mind.
The true God is not one thing or an ideal or a person or a practice or an imagination or anything physical in nature or even an experience for that matter.

The God or the creator can never be experienced with *division*, *separation*, or *illusion* that the mind creates. This is very subtle and requires work to be very observant to actually *see* that there is *nothing to observe* and that there is no difference between *who* is observing and *what* is being observed.

When one sees this in actuality, the illusion of separation ends, the mind stops dividing, and the search for God ends, too. We see that there is nothing else to refer to as God as you are a part of it, too, as is everything else.

No words, no explanations, no religion, no preachings, no teachings, no leader, no sect, no tradition, no philosophy, and no human creation—physical or of the mind—can ever let you *be* in this unending moment.

The closest a human can be to the creator is by *being* in the unending moment.

~

Lesson 8 — You are Humanity.

We can't have it all.

A rich person cannot know the poor ways.
A poor man cannot know the lavish lifestyle.

We cannot directly see with our eyes or hear with our ears a man who is far away from us.
One cannot be at peace until the nature of existence is looked at.
One cannot fly a plane and drive a car at the same time.

No two humans can occupy the same physical space at once.

One can't be thinking of something and not be that.

There is a limit to what a human can do. That's the nature of life.

But there is also when a human is not limited because then there is a merging of himself and the rest of the universe. They become one.

It is also the same when a human perceives, actually perceives not through his limited senses but perception beyond it, where he realizes he is no different than all the human beings in the world.

He realizes deeply that what he feels and thinks is no different than any particular human. They will have different situations, but the resulting human experiences are the same.

The whole of humanity is one.
You are humanity.

~

CHAPTER II — EARTHLY BODY.

Lesson 9 — You Are an Organism, First.

We forget the simple fact that we are a consequence of an amalgamation of 78 organs that came together over billions of years to function the way they do in the very body that we have today. This fundamental lack of understanding and forgetting the basis of our physical reality has led us to extremes of polluting and overusing the resources of Mother Earth.

It is essential to come back to the senses of our body or, so to say, become conscious of one's body. Indian culture, for example, has long emphasized the importance of connecting with the nature around us through yoga. When learned from a genuine teacher, yoga enables one to engage with the external environment through the body.

When an individual becomes aware and realizes that they genuinely have an earthly body, it brings about an incredible shift in perspective. This shift, in turn, changes how people approach their everyday lives—how they eat, consume, live healthily, stay in sync with nature, avoid waste of natural resources, and promote awareness of our fragile environment.

You are an organism:

None of the bodily activities are under our control. Even breathing seems like something we do, but it happens on its own, too. Our only control is over the breathing speed, without any choice about starting or stopping it.

+ We can move, but the movements of what lies beneath the skin are not in our control.

+ We can walk, but the functioning of our legs is beyond our control.

+ We can eat, but the taste and recognition of the food happens without our control.

+ We can drink water, but the movement of it and how big a role it plays within the body is totally out of our reach.

+ We can sleep, but the dreams that come are not within our control.

+ We can bathe, but the vitality within each cell is not in our hands.

+ We can sit, but the curvature and alignment that allow you to sit are not in our control.

+ We can poop, but digestion is not under our control.

+ We can have sex, but the hormones involved are not in our control.

+ We can see, but cannot control the processing of images.

+ We can hear, but the interpretation of what we hear is not in our grasp.

+ We can touch, but the sensations experienced are not in our control.

+ We can take drugs, but how they affect us internally is not regulated by our will.

There is nothing that we, as the mover of our own body, can control. Everything that makes us human has been set to function in specific ways long ago to allow us to live everyday life. Those with disabilities still live as the body manages itself without falling apart. Regarding the body, the only choice and control we have is food. What one eats, how many times one eats, when one eats, and how much one eats—these are controllable. Apart from this, there is no control over everything else about the body from the beginning.

+ Your body was taken out to come into this world, and you did not have a choice. Your body will die, and you still won't have a choice.

+ Your physical body is a result of two organisms—your biological parents—coming together.

+ Your siblings and family members are organisms, too.

+ Your friends and colleagues are organisms, too.

+ Your partner is an organism as well.

+ All the people you have in your life and the world are organisms, too. This is the united physical reality that we experience.

Now, the fact is that the body ages. As it is a physical entity, the way we maintain our body and, with the effect of time— the functions and activities of the cells, tissues, organs, systems, and body as a whole start to depreciate. This is bound to happen no matter how much science tries to extend the life span of a body. The physical body is governed by what we have worded as the mind. The brain is responsible as the central point of all activities, but it is the mind that defines the very way a person ends up living and the quality of it. It is a paradox of how the person shapes their mind and precisely how the mind will shape their life.

The loop can only stop once the person realizes that he himself is feeding his mind, which, in turn, shapes his quality of life. Although the body is an independent entity by itself, in our experience, it doesn't exist independently. Without the Earth's atmosphere, humans would not exist. Without the support of plants that started generating oxygen millions of years ago, there wouldn't be breathable oxygen for humans today.

Breath is one such force that connects our body to the rest of the outside world. This means that humans are not isolated but intertwined with everything else. While they may be confined to a particular location, they remain intimately connected to the entire world. However, they often fail to experience this intimacy and love because they are unaware of it. As we hail from a planet called Earth, we belong to it, and it is our true home. We have always lived and died here.

This is where we come from and return to. The components of our bodies, as of today, 2024, originate from Mother Earth. We were shaped to exist within the safety of our home, which is why astronauts need to wear suits when they venture into space. These suits allow them to survive beyond their natural home on Earth. No matter where humans go, it will never be a natural home for them, as they will consistently have to maintain a similar kind of safety that Mother Earth provides them without any effort. Just like you and me, there are other organisms in this home. We are one of millions of organisms living on our beautiful planet. Because of our sharp intellect, we, as a species, have become the most dominant, and hence, we are spread out in almost all corners of our home.

However, we can never truly understand the views of other organisms. We may comprehend, but it won't reflect how they experience life, be it organisms on Earth or on different planets. This limitation makes it impossible to see the wholeness of life through human experiences since those experiences are distinctly human and do not apply universally.

To see something that is beyond the human organism, one must completely accept that this body is an organism that experiences life and has its own limitations when it comes to perceiving the truth. But at the same time, there is something beyond the body, beyond the mind or so to say behind what makes us human, behind what unites all of humanity, behind what makes everything exist to keep ticking without a purpose or meaning, and behind all creation.

You have the same flesh and bones as the rest of the 8.2 Billion people! It took me a long time to realize that the other 8.2 Billion people do the same thing as I do. We have the same body with variations based on our birthplace. Whether living in a so-called developed country, in a developing one, or even on Mars, you still have the same process that all humans go through daily.

+ You breathe

+ You feel

+ You touch

+ You smell

+ You hear

+ You see

+ You talk

+ You eat

+ You argue

+ You fight

+ You win

+ You lose

+ You hesitate

+ You work

+ You run

+ You walk

+ You support

+ You love

+ You fail

+ You cry

+ You explore

+ You try again

+ You fall down
+ You think
+ You forget
+ You remember
+ You believe
+ You sit
+ You sleep
+ You bathe
+ You procreate
+ You excrete
+ You heal
+ You ponder
+ You reflect
+ You achieve
+ You let go
+ You discover
+ You introspect
+ You question
+ You act
+ You get rich
+ You lose it all
+ You get depressed
+ You drive
+ You learn
+ You enjoy
+ You play
+ You help

+ You give

+ You take

+ You look

+ You connect

+ You nurture

+ You cherish

+ You perceive

+ You experience

+ You regret

+ You empathize

+ You spend

+ You earn

+ You read

+ You write

+ You listen

+ You taste

+ You stumble

+ You grow

+ You inspire

+ You lead

+ You expand

+ You recover

+ You fear

+ You die

+ You embrace

+ You exist

+ You pursue

+ You understand

+ You encourage

+ You overcome

+ You seek

+ You challenge

+ You influence

+ You fulfill

+ You relate

+ You wonder

+ You create

+ You transform

When all of this you do is what the rest of humanity does, too, where is the question of whether any person is separate from you?
The separation is physically bodied individually, but the mechanisms that are there in all of us are essentially the same.

The body is *one* of the creations of the creator that took a long, long time to be what you see yourself embodied in.

You embody the body.

There is depth in these words.

You embody the body, but there is no separation between you and the body.

A logical mind will read that statement and instantly divide it into two because that's what it is designed for. It just functions out of what it is created for and exists for. However, logic to understand that you embody the body will not work as the logic ends here, and the mind cannot grasp it to make sense. And this is where something beyond the contents and nature of the mind takes place.

You know you have this body of yours because you can feel and see it with the view you have from your eyes. There is no other place other than your body that you have experienced or will ever experience anything. This is your physical limitation, but it also comes with a capacity to experience and perceive everything beyond its physical limitations, too.

When this understanding of a lack of control over the body's internal mechanisms and functions arises, it inevitably prompts a person to reflect on the larger picture of the world and what truly matters. At its core, breathing is a fundamental necessity for all humans. The realization that our breathing is not an isolated event but rather exists in a symbiotic relationship with the trees and nature around us brings a quality of simplicity that is immensely significant in fostering change at the root level, shaping how we as individuals navigate our lives on this planet.

CHAPTER III — HUMAN INSIGHT.

Lesson 10 — Ocean of Humanity.

People who function solely based on an external activity will not know balance. This lack of balance and not being in sync with their nature of being is what causes them to be in turmoil internally. Unless it is addressed there is no way to not suffer.

What we call the mind is like the "Ocean of Humanity." Water that crashes into the shore and the water that is ever so in motion in the middle of the ocean are one and the same.

The space where the thoughts rise and fall is mankind's collective space of existence.

Not your space or my space, but the space of all human beings who ever lived before, who are living now, and all those who are going to come into existence. If only you could see the beauty of this space.

All human beings come with it because it is everyone's, not yours and not mine. It is our space of being. Nothing more has been or ever will be known outside of this.

One person's contents of the mind will not be the same as another, but it is this space of **Nilness** that all of humanity arises from. That is where it is ever so in motion, swaying, living, and dying effortlessly. That which rises and falls, from an apparently individual mind, gives meaning to it all.

The combined existence of both, the source of creation and the creation itself, is the illusion and reality existing at every moment.

It is quite easy to live an entire life without ever questioning any of it. Without ever questioning the way of living. It is only a matter of having a few objectives to accomplish that would take a major portion of a human lifespan. That suffices to be busy in life without ever having to question what it is all about —without ever wanting to dwell into the beauty of the core of existing—and just be content with the comfort, certainties, and security of a rather long, satisfying life.

But those few people to whom the suffering of what it is all about keeps returning and doesn't go away with superficial accomplishments, these few people will look deeper into their lives.

Those who start questioning everything and everyone in their life will begin to see a shift in their outlook of what it is to be human, only if they do it without a personal agenda of their own to reach somewhere or attain something.

The experience of the change in paradigm is subjective, but there is a perception that one arrives at that changes it all. That perception can never be put into human words because it is not an experience, for an experience requires sensations tangled with memories and knowledge.

When there is a complete ending of accumulated identities, beliefs, memories, knowledge, and even experiences, then and only then can a human reach a sanctity outside the space of being and touch **Nilness**, where there is nothing at all. Here is where there is an end to all human suffering.

And here, be.

The rise and fall in the ocean of humanity can then be looked at with **Nilness** as the foundation and not the mind.

~

Lesson 11 — The Illusion of Peace of Mind.

Concepts we create for our understanding are taken as facts, which is a completely false way of looking at life.

If you don't understand what the mind truly is, finding peace within it is like trying to breathe underwater—it's simply not possible. The pursuit of peace within the confines of our own mind, frankly, is absurd.

To seek peace while trapped in the thoughts is akin to trying to swim while gasping for air. One needs to transcend this medium to breathe freely. Similarly, to comprehend or take charge of the mind, one must go beyond it.

The domain of the mind:

The mind dictates every aspect of our lives—our actions, thoughts, decisions, and experiences.

When you're engulfed by your thoughts, everything you do originates from this mental clutter. This isn't just theory; it's as real as the sky or the ocean.

The challenge?

We're too entangled in our thoughts to notice. But there's a way to step outside of this mental maze.

+ Observation.

+ Looking.

+ Seeing.

+ Attention.

Choose any term, but remember, in true observation, there are no words, no clutter. Here, the mind can try to pull you back into its chaos, but with conscious observation, it fails.

This is the truth. *The compulsive mind cannot coexist with reality.*

Yet, through diligent inner work, the mind can come to a place where it lives in symbiosis with reality. This is the truth. *The conscious mind coexists with reality.*

This journey isn't for the faint-hearted. If you think external efforts are demanding, try this inner exploration. The energy you expend to see, to truly see the mind's activity, eclipses any physical endeavor.

Freedom from the mind:

The concept of being free from the mind while using it as needed baffles many—confusion is a game of the mind.

Reality isn't confused. It is constant, needing no validation. But to truly perceive this timelessness, to live it daily, is beyond the mind's comprehension. In this state of reality, the mind loses its grip, releasing you from the bounds of time.

Embracing timelessness:

When you are fully present, you touch an essence of timelessness, merging with the vastness of existence. This perception, beyond words or the mind's grasp, introduces you to **Nilness**—a profound simplicity where you dance with the truth, embodying the whole of humanity in that moment of pure awareness.

~

Lesson 12 — Interpretations.

Born as humans, the ability to interpret, record, and pass on information is what made us dominate the planet we come out of. But one needs to see that the mind interprets all the time, which is as much a boon as it is a severe addiction that most are not aware of. I call interpreting everything an addiction because it ticks all the boxes.

Interpreting everything that one comes across is necessary at the early stages of life. But after a certain point, if the person who is doing the interpretation has lost control of when and how much to do it, that shows a compulsive engagement. It then becomes a pattern that tends to be difficult to identify in the first place.

Even a dialogue between two people has interpretations by each that are different from one another.

Just as *an alcoholic has no control* and gets hooked to the drinks *for its taste and numbing the pain—the mind that is functioning without any control of the person to whom it belongs to* gets hooked to interpreting all that occurs *for reasserting what it already knows as a belief or fear*.

Let me rephrase and repeat for those who did not get it or find it hard to correlate the two:

+ An alcoholic has no control = The mind that is functioning without any control of the person it belongs to.

+ An alcoholic gets hooked to the drinks = The mind that gets hooked to interpreting all that occurs.

+ An alcoholic drinks for its taste and numbing the pain = The mind keeps interpreting for reasserting what it already knows as a belief or fear.

As this takes place, where there is always interpretation happening in the mind through thinking, in order to re-establish the patterns that the mind already has learned until then, the same gets repeated over and over and over again. Such a compulsively repetitive mind does not allow space for silence to seep in as it is constantly at work.

What this does to a person over a number of years is he loses control over what, how, and when they need to "use their thinking ability."

I cannot stress "use their thinking ability" enough. People do use thinking, but that comes out of compulsiveness rather than by choice.

Using their thinking ability by choice is where there is ultimate freedom to have a free mind.
A free mind is one where the person *thinks* when he wants to.
A free mind is one where there is no difference in thinking and reality.

Thinking then is not separate from the person. This has to be realized and is possible only with brutal honesty and sincerity to be aware of one's own thoughts, moment-to-moment, by looking at their thoughts, which makes it seem different at first, but this is useful to see that what is being thought about ceases when it is being looked at and observed with *total attention.*

The thinking ceases because the person is *paying attention* to his own thinking. One might then ask, "Who is paying attention to even look at what is being thought?"—This, my friend, is still the play of the mind that is always designed to split and see as *two entities*, whereas in reality, there is no two but the mind cannot stop doing what it has been designed naturally to do by the existence and there is no way you and I can stop it from fulfilling its purpose just as much as you and I do not want to die physically. Without falling into the trap of stopping the thoughts, a simple approach of observing without questioning who is looking produces the most obvious answer that only you can perceive, as nobody else can do it for you.

The thinking ceases as it is not separate from the person. Please *do not interpret* this as the person is his thoughts. If such a misinterpretation happens in the very lesson of interpretation, that would certainly be a debacle.

A person *thinks*, which itself makes thinking and the activities of the mind something that the person *must* have hold over. Hold, not by force or control, but by a choice that comes with choicelessness, voluntarily. Without any resistance.

The mind is a mere tool but a sharp one to be used rather than the tool engulfing and becoming the person.

The subtleties of the mind can only be observed when the person brings *awareness* to the obsessive mind, which provides it the much-required space for silence to not interpret when it is not needed.

To clarify—

You are doing the thinking. The thinking doesn't just happen to you out of thin air. The thinking happens wherever you go, which means what? It only signifies that the thinking moves with you, and *in that moment of thinking, you are the thought*! Then the thought is over, and you are not it. There is an ongoing play in this unending moment, which is the most beautiful game of life.

~

Lesson 13 — Patterns.

More often than we realize, we tend to limit our capabilities, which eventually affects the quality of our lives, by self-imposed limitations. This happens either through experience of our own or others, and we stick with it as if it is the only way to be.

We get attached to such identities in more ways than we can imagine, as these are very subtle patterns that grow in intensity over a period of time but are not easily identifiable as they become a default in the way we function on a day-to-day basis.

Such patterns can be recognized when it comes to the surface, but usually, they remain in the background, playing a commanding role—

+ In the decisions we make.

+ The lifestyle we live.

+ The mindset we cultivate.

+ The quality of relationships with self and other people.

+ The work that we do.

+ And more importantly, in our growth as a human being.

Unless these patterns that are not helping us—acting as the hidden barriers to living a content life—are allowed to rise to the surface for them to be first seen and then acted upon consciously, there will remain that feeling and actuality that makes us unfulfilled in many areas of life.

Allowing the sustenance of such unaided patterns is not only the most dangerous thing to do over the course of a lifetime, but it also does not allow the individual to realize life and existence as a whole and carve out a life that could have been lived consciously without all of the sufferings.

Lesson 14 — From Primal Fear to Peaceful Presence.

We inherit this biological body from our parents. But there are inheritances we have received that date back to millions of years ago.

In those days of human evolution, it was all about survival.

+ Survival for food.

+ Survival from others.

+ Survival from animals.

+ Survival from weather.

+ Survival for living.

This gave rise to the sense of protecting ourselves. Protecting ourselves means having defense mechanisms in place to avoid being hungry, hurt, killed, sick, or dead. While it was being cultivated, inevitably, each ended up having their own ways of defending themselves and had no other means than raising their levels of defense as per the danger and situations. *This is the root of the dominancy that we all have today.* This is where it actually started, millions of years ago. It is not something we happened to pick up from our parents. It is inherently there evolutionarily in all humans.

Being dominant is necessary when the situation demands, but there is no need to *stick* with the idea that we are dominant by nature or personality. We are not. It is the situations that make us dominant and defend ourselves, even if it is a verbal defense or at a deeper level of thinking.

What we are by nature is Nil. And by that, I mean, at a deeper level, we as human beings are devoid of the ideas and all the illusions we have generated to understand the functioning of ourselves and the world.

The human thought processes and all the creations that come out of it require the past or *time* to exist, but *existence is void of time* itself because it is alive and throbbing in this very instance all the time.

But since the body that we do have today has deeply absorbed the behaviors of our early humans, it cannot be thrown out of the system just like that and requires *tremendous attention & presence* to be able to look at behaviors such as dominancy when it is not necessary or comes out of compulsiveness.

The understanding itself that our day-to-day dominant reactions have roots as far as our early ancestors who lived not thousands but millions of years ago, is sometimes enough to remember at times when this behaviour comes out. The more one recognizes that they indeed do have dominant traits, identifies them, and goes deeper to work it out, the more the chances of eliminating the deeply rooted ancestral behavior that still exists within our body and mind.

For our early ancestors, there was no need or the time to think about realizing the truth as the basic necessities were of primal importance. They were totally involved in making ends meet. But today, most of us do not have such a dire need for survival.

+ Survival for food is not a problem in the modern world that we are in. A lot actually gets wasted. Since you are reading this book, it is highly unlikely that food is an issue. Only the decision of what to eat seems to be more of an issue among those who have it a lot.

+ Survival from others has drastically reduced with the enforcement of laws and securities in place. The threats we do face from others are most likely a product of living unconsciously.

+ Survival from animals is not something we are in danger of today in the urban world as compared to how it was millions of years ago. Now, it exists mostly in the wilderness or when the animals come over for a visit since their natural habitats are taken away by us.

+ Survival from the weather is why most of us have a roof over us and many of the luxuries that our early ancestors did not have the privilege of. Yes, even that chair you are sitting on and the air conditioner that is running in your room is a privilege. Our ancestors sat on stones and waited for winter.

+ Survival for living in the modern world today is majorly based on earning for our day-to-day necessities. This, too, is done with comfort taken into account, starting from the place that you work, the systems that you follow, the benefits that you get, and the rights that come with all kinds of work today.

The very reason that you are reading this today on the internet is a privilege itself, as information relaying at such a speed and proportion is a luxury in itself. The very reason that you have the time right now to read this information proves that your survival needs are taken care of, and you have the luxury of spending time to read information for your growth.

The next time you react in a dominant way to the people around you, notice the emotions that run incessantly within you. This is causing havoc to your own system, to begin with. Even the toughest of situations can be handled with a calm response and conversation. When you respond calmly to a person who is angry, they do not expect that because they are expecting an angry and a fight response due to the evolutionary behavior that we have inherited without choice.

It is a proven technique to take a break and walk away from such a heated situation as it reduces its intensity, and when you come back later, the matter at hand can be dealt with in a more stable manner.

The next time you react angrily to your parents, your partner, your colleagues, somebody on the street, or even to yourself in the form of thinking:

+ Come to an observation that you are *reacting compulsively*.

+ When there is this observation, a realization of "I am acting out of anger" or "I am acting out of dominancy" takes place—a realization of it and not the worded-out thoughts.

+ The reaction and, with it, the negative thinking ceases in a few moments after such an in-the-moment realization, depending on how conscious the person is.

Realize that anger and dominancy are traits that do not go well within our system itself and, 99.99% of the time, aren't required. When it is shown to other people, it creates an entire environment of toxicity, which disrupts the stability of others and our own.

Most of the people are only surviving and dragging themselves to live in fear constantly.

Very few actually live with love being the base of their life.

When love is the foundation of one's existence, there is beauty in such a life. Such beauty cannot be seen by a person who holds fear as a way of living.

If we do indeed want stability in our lives, then we wouldn't want to bring instability in any way. With this drive to be stable, there comes an *innate power of observation and looking at all of our actions, behaviors, and thinking.* This can become our most vital ally in the journey of self-discovery & awareness.

Lesson 15 — Darkness.

The power of darkness is such that it can linger around, defining a person's moment-to-moment actions and perception to a point where the individual is driven by it. This can be sensed in that little moment where they talk out of their pattern, which is their darkness, and there is a subtle joy on their face as if they are getting a kick out of negativity.

That, my friend, is the power of the dark side.

It can engulf a person whole and wrap them with a gift of negativity, which they live by without ever questioning the nature of such a gift.

The dark side is the enemy, but the enemy is not on the outside.

The enemy is part of you residing within the realm of the mind. This is why no matter what you do or say, the problems never go away if it is handled externally, since the root of the resulting chaos is within you.

The mind is not the enemy, but our addiction to the contents of the mind is.

To come to the realization that a man needs to work on himself to resolve his inner and outer conflicts, years and decades pass by. This is why the sooner an individual comes to recognize that the problem has never been on the outside, there will arrive that zeal and drive to work on oneself.

When this happens deliberately, that man has embarked on his spiritual journey.

~

Lesson 16 — Psychological Knowledge.

What one talks about comes out only from the space of knowledge. The knowledge that they picked up. It can only be about themselves as those particular patterns of knowledge have been picked up depending on a number of factors—the source of it, the interpretation while absorbing the information, and especially the state of mind the person is in, which includes the emotions, life situations, age, etc.

Very few know to listen and not be there as a stack of memories. To not sit there as a bundle of memories on top of which the interpretations and experiences are built upon.

Yes, we do require the information, but there is no need to function as a human being with the baggage of years and decades of knowledge.

The mind deeply stores and retains the experiences we have had in childhood and starts building all the meanings out of the knowledge that it has retained deeply.

The priorities that you give to a certain thing today have been defined long ago when your personality was being shaped while devising coping mechanisms for all things and people that caused insecurity to you.

The negative basis of such coping mechanisms is based on knowledge and experiences we have already had and it becomes hard to look back in order to find the first starting point as to where it started for the meanings we do have today.

The backdoor to find out—the root cause of our meanings, the reasons why we prioritize certain aspects of life more than others, and the automated interpretations one tends to have— lies in the revelations of the mind itself. The patterns of the mind cannot function in the background always, and at certain times, there are flashes of images or memories that come upon us, at times when we are doing something. These flashes or unintended reflections or memories take us back to the root of where the action you are indulging in the moment comes from.

For example:

We may have parents who are secretive about what they say so that others do not hear them. If this has been a childhood experience, then the mind copies that from the parent as a behavior, and one tends to do the same in some aspects of their life.

Through such a pattern that is not yours, whenever you begin to question, for example, "Why don't I like to speak out loud?", the flashes of your parent with the remembrance of a memory where you might have seen them do such secretive talking will pop up in the mind. That is the root. It shows up in the mind because *a pattern cannot exist without having started somewhere.* For the mind to go out executing a pattern, it needs to access the knowledge and the information such a pattern is based and built upon, and only then can you, as the continuer of the pattern, go on repeating your parent's patterns without ever realizing it.

Unless you question why you do what you do.

The beauty of using a fresh mind to question—without thinking —why it does what it does, invites presence into it which is powerful to take you to the root of the psychological knowledge.

When you do question and observe these flashes of memories whilst or after doing a certain action, thinking, or behavior— in the very observation of the root, there is a possibility of the pattern dissolving. This also depends on how deeply the pattern has been ingrained.

Now, isn't that beautiful? The mind has patterns and acts out of them, but it also provides a backdoor to get rid of the patterns.

One need not look at all the knowledge they have as information as if it is something to be proud of. If one does that, then it only strengthens the attachment to knowledge.

To see the reality for yourself, the psychological knowledge that the mind has accumulated has no place at all. It only acts as a barrier to the truth of life.

When you look at a tree or clouds as they are, there must be a deep silence without the filters of the mind, which are present in the form of knowledge. If you look through the filters of the mind, you see an adulterated view of reality corrupted by knowledge.

There is a deeper way to live a life where knowledge has its place. Its usage has to be by choice, not by compulsive activity of the mind, where it keeps hindering your view of reality.

Lesson 17 — Vicious Cycle.

Parents who are unconscious decide to have kids out of sheer pressure from society or to fulfill one of their many egoistic desires. In the first few years of this child's upbringing, where he is supposed to have an environment of safety and love, ends up taking parents and other people's toxicity with no fault of his own, with no control over what input he is absorbing. Though now it can be spoken in hindsight as years, those actual years when this child is being exposed to his family's unconsciousness are experienced as though that is the only way the world outside of him works.

The behavior, the reactions of the parents, and the scenes that the child sees—be it the good, the bad, or the ugly—get engraved deeply at a crucial phase of the growth of the child's understanding and development of how to be and cope outside of the womb. The womb was the only place where he felt the safest before being bombarded with the toxicity of unconscious people.

That child does not have the innate ability yet to choose what he lets in and what he does not.

I find the analogy of the sun very intriguing to what an infant faces in those initial years of childhood. It is very similar to the ability that we, as outgrowths of this planet, do not have over the sunlight.

The sun shines no matter what. No matter if we humans exist on this planet or not. No matter if the plants get too much of it. No matter what lives or what dies on this planet. The sun keeps shining as it is its innate design to keep doing so. The "Children of Earth" *need* the sunshine to exist. There is a nurturing connection between the two. The "Children of Earth" have no choice but to receive all that the sun comes with, all of its sunshine. In the same way, the fragile and innocent child has no *choice* but to receive *all* that his parents come with.

This is a fact that is fixed in stone for the rest of the child's life, irrespective of the adult version of the child ever discovering the impact they both have in his day-to-day life. It is a fact that his parent's principles, ideologies, beliefs, ego, philosophy, approach, understanding, opinions, patterns, learnings, dreams, desires, personality, attachments, regrets, goals, perspectives, emotions, values, behaviors, thinking, and way of living—*becomes his!* There is no question about it.

Sink that in for a few minutes.

Read it again and again because most of our life, we may end up living the symbiotic effects of our parents.

On the bright side—if you turn to the *awareness* that continual partaking in this parental symbiosis leads to no individuality of your own and is no more than a revised replica of your parent's life and their take on life, you will realize that you *now*, as an adult, have the innate ability to choose what to let in and what not to—even if it is from the past.

You can now understand where your parents came from psychologically and dissect all of their limitations, which they ended up sharing with you for a long period. These limitations have gotten so deeply engraved that *distinguishing what is theirs and what is yours becomes the most important work of your adulthood and the rest of your life.* This is by no means a matter to be taken lightly.

The only question here is—Are you open enough to see that you have lived a major portion of life thinking it is your way of living but, in fact, have subtly lived the very way your parents have lived and even more so with your own set of additions?

If you decide to look at it deeply and work on it with complete honesty, there is a chance for this cycle to end. Otherwise, the vicious cycle and the presence of parents' influences continue *in you* and get passed on to the next generations.

~

Lesson 18 — The Paradox of Security.

The mind is repetitive in nature. It lives and thrives with repetitive actions. Its innate nature is cyclical, as is for everything in life. There is security in repetitive actions for the mind. There is no security for the mind in the freedom from being repetitive.

Security is the basis of holding on to the past. Now, why does the mind depend so much on the past to be programmed?

The mind has evolved by wanting security for a thousand different reasons outwardly. It is this need to be secure that the mind continuously seeks security in all of its contents. The song that we keep playing out one after the other and the same lyrics played out hundreds if not thousands of times for years is the repetitive nature of the mind. You like the song, that is another matter, but the mind will keep repeating all of its contents in some way or the other to fulfill its design and natural functioning to exist with all its content. All of it.

There is repetition of all sorts that happens in the mind. The repetitions that keep playing out of nowhere when you are not consciously thinking is the mind not allowing you to be in this unending moment. It opposes it because its contents cannot exist when one *is* in the unending moment. The mind plays out a song, a memory, an experience, or some other information, and it is in the mind's survival nature to not allow you to be still, which in turn allows you to be in this unending moment. It functions this way because the mind is like a child that wants your attention all the time. It functions this way because it operates *in time*.

The mind can only exist with time. The mind has no existence without the psychological time that it itself has created. And in the same way if something created us humans, the creation that we are cannot be separate or different from the creator itself.

Time is a creation of the mind. If time is a creation of the mind, it also means that time and the mind cannot exist separately. They are one and the same. One can actually experiment on themselves to see the fact of this.

The past is time. The future is the projection of past information and memories. Both require time. But as there is no time in this unending moment, the mind cannot survive to continue playing out its contents or, so to say, the functioning of the mind ends in the unending moment as it requires time to exist. The unending moment is devoid of the time created by the human mind.

The ending of time and the mind are not different. The ending of the mind is in the stillness of this unending moment where there is no time, where the contents of the mind are not playing out.

The only solution that nobody in the world talks about is to allow the mind itself to see this danger for the very way it functions repetitively. *As the mind is designed to seek security, once there is clear and pure perception, and it sees the paradox that its activities of repeating over and over again is itself dangerous, it moves away from it.*

But this is a deep observation and requires one to be totally present with the repetitions of the mind as it happens. You must become aware of its activities.

Anything physical that is subjected to iterations becomes damaged over a period of time. The brain is physical and is interconnected to the realm of the mind, which is not physical. But as the brain in our body is physical, it gets damaged due to the repetitions caused by the programming. When there is a deep perception that the mind is programmed, and in that programming, there is no security whatsoever, this perception itself ends the repetitiveness.

When there are no more compulsive repetitions of the mind, the brain itself begins to physically renew, and there will be the mind that looks at everything freshly where security has its place only when necessary.

~

CHAPTER IV — HUMAN RELATIONSHIPS.
Lesson 19 — Conflicts.

+ Why do couples and family members fight?
+ Why do colleagues argue at work?
+ Why are most people in the world fighting?
+ Why do people have conflicts?
+ *Why are you fighting with yourself?*

Asking these questions is the first part of getting into the seriousness of so much misery in the world that humans have created among and within themselves. How can you fight with yourself? To fight, there needs to be two people. Are you two people within yourself, or are you one human being? Ask these questions in the most serious manner possible because being light-hearted about it does not allow you to dig out the dirt that is hiding away the truth.

Two people can get into the most arduous and nasty conflicts. What essentially takes place is they get identified with the memories of one another, be it a partner, a boss, or a parent. After knowing the person for a while, the mind gets fixated on their patterns and does an excellent job of keeping those memories alive while dealing with that person in a heated situation.

No matter how much or what you might have done for that person in the past, it doesn't make any difference because the mind even has the capability to take all that is apparently good and turn it on its head to make it look like it was bad. It changes it according to the present emotions and situation we tend to be in with that person so that the already set patterns can be validated and re-affirmed for the mind to function in a similar way when a future situation arises.

All this does is only dig the mind deeper into being identified with that sort of pattern, and the same keeps repeating as default *unless* the person becomes aware that this is happening repeatedly, and he looks at it to question it since it has not been serving him in any way.

People go crazy defending themselves so much that it becomes impossible at a later stage to realize that this is even happening. To recognize a self-created pattern is so simple. You just have to *look* at:

+ How do you think?
+ What do you think?
+ How do you react?
+ What do you react to?
+ How do you behave in scenarios with other people?

Observe. Look at your own patterns. There is no point looking at other people and their behaviors as it doesn't matter at all. Those are *their* behaviors. You cannot ever get into their mind to control any darn thing. You cannot change any person because that's what they are, that's what you have got to work with. Take difficult situations and people as an *opportunity* to first force yourself to look at the mind, and then gradually, it becomes second nature to instantly see that *how* or *what* another human is talking about is *all* about themselves. It has always been about themselves.

It has never been about you. It is *their* thinking.

Conflicts are unavoidable as two people cannot have the exact same views or way of thinking even if they are brought up in the same environment. Expecting two people who meet in their 20s and thereafter to not have differing opinions, principles, and values is one's blindness to the reality of how things are.

Wake up to the reality of yourself and other people. First, see your own reality, the reality of the mind, and become free of it in order to have no separation whatsoever from reality itself. Then, everything else becomes crystal clear, and one can start creating life consciously by choice.

~

Lesson 20 — Love.

Love is what *you* feel inside you.

It is that unseeable force that gives you butterflies for other lives.

Love is what you generate to get back up.

It is what gives you a tingling sensation when thinking of life.

Love and life are the ocean and the waves.

Love is what overcomes the lack of love.

Love is the sun shining upon our home without forgetting.

Love is my eyes looking at the sky, the clouds, the mountains,

And not knowing how it was all made and why.

Love is simply being in awe of the space that allows so much to be in it.

Love is also that which takes away and still throbs in you and me.

Lesson 21 — Unconditional Love.

When someone listens to you, it does not mean that you own them.

There are a whole lot of people acting out of fear, and then there are these few people with unconditional love in their hearts who can spend their entire lives giving away their time and efforts to *shower* their love to dear ones *through* their actions or words. And these are usually our parents who, if they happen to have unconditional love in any form, will forgive anything their children would do or say. Though, it's not completely a healthy way to always be forgiving to a child which then gives him an impression that it is alright to do anything he wishes to, which is a recipe for disaster as he grows up.

When such a person with pure love in their heart listens to you and always comes back no matter how harsh you are to them, know it deep in your being that such kind of love is the rarest today in this modern world, and you need not make a mockery out of it by taking their presence and actions in your life for granted.

When they won't be around anymore, and if you continue taking such pure-hearted people for granted and keep treating them badly, what you did to them will be a lifelong regret that you will not be able to do much about. The only thing you *can* do is, while they are still around, *look* at them as if you have no *image* of them. By no image, I mean look at them with no memory of *all* that *you* have built up over the years about that person.

Drop them.

And when you look with such a fresh view that is not corrupted by the filters of the mind, that is when you are truly with that person. *That* is the only time you can connect and be with that person here and now to see how much love they have in all the small and big things they do for you.

When you see this kind of love that has no boundaries, you are bound to get soaked with unconditional love, and then there will finally be a sharing that comes out of pure love from you, too. But for any of this to happen, one needs to be vulnerable about everything—to themselves and others.

Lesson 22 — Looking Without Memory.

When you look at your partner without any knowledge or memory or information about what you already know, there arrives a looking that has no time in it.

First of all, it is difficult for many people to actually do this with their partner because they know them too much.

If one can keep their partner's memory aside, there would be no problem in any relationship in the world. The problem is that it has become impossible to keep that memory or image of that person aside, even for a minute. We have come to such a place since both have an unconscious mind. When two people are unconscious, the dramas that build up and unfold over the years are unbelievable.

The root cause of all conflicts is not realizing who you are.

How can one be loving for the long term when the couple has kept building images of one another?

What relationship problem can they really solve when they do not know the root cause itself?

The root cause of all relationship problems is *unawareness*. To be aware of:

+ Oneself.

+ The activities of their thoughts.

+ The way the mind is functioning or fluctuating on a day-to-day basis.

+ The habits that have been developed unconsciously.

+ The default reactions to anything and everything.

+ The constant need to be stimulated.

+ The repressed emotions.

+ The personality that is at play.

Being aware of these brings a *drastic* change in the quality of relationships that we have with ourselves and others.

The more you are aware of yourself, the more you become aware of others.

~

Lesson 23 — Trauma.

The root of all prevailing traumas in adulthood is unawareness.

When looked at from one perspective, human life is all about being aware of what has happened to us in unawareness.

Having a partner who is a mirror to you is so necessary. One must be very grateful to have a partner who is ready to help while you get through your traumas.

Traumas are deeply embedded in the mind of a person. When the parents and people who brought the child up were not stable themselves, that person's childhood is so traumatic that they hardly remember where their current behaviors and patterns have roots in.

Childhood is when a human is fundamentally programmed and becomes an outcome of *all* that he has experienced.

All of it. Nothing spared.

Those experiences become his framework to build his life upon and the traumas that the child faced in his infancy reveal themselves in intimate relationships in adulthood.

The way he conducts the relationship, respects the partner, behaves, thinks, and does everything in the relationship is in *accord* with what he was programmed as a child.

~

Lesson 24 — Boundaries.

One needs to have boundaries with another person to not let them run all over. But the paradox is that there is no boundary in reality.

In reality, your boundary does not end with the extent of this body that you have. It goes beyond that, which is why there is air from the outside that can be taken in and let out.

This is why there can be actions on the outside, the beginnings of which are on the inside.

Which is why the entire inner body mechanisms are dependent on the food and the air that we intake from the outside.

If the body was a closed system, it would collapse in a matter of few seconds.

Your body is not a closed system. It is one that connects and thrives only because it co-exists with the materials it needs from the outside.

If you have never realized this before, I am happy to be the one sharing the news that the boundaries of all the countries in the world do not exist in reality. Borders of countries are those that we humans have put because of our differences. These boundaries do not exist in reality.

There is no separation in reality. To see the purest form of this, the forest and nature are prime examples where all the birds, all the animals, all the flowers, and all the creation of nature co-exist without any boundary.

~

Lesson 25 — Comparison.

Have you found yourself comparing yourself with another person? That you do not know this thing. He seems to know a lot more than you. She is more beautiful than I am. How does he make so much money? Is she good enough for me? Why isn't he normal like the others? She's so much prettier. Look at that house. Why can't you be like him?

All these and millions of others have the foundation laid with a reference of another.

What is the need to compare?

Comparison takes place when there are a lot of options to choose from. In the modern world that we live in, there is no shortage of options. With the advent of the internet and everything becoming so convenient with a tap of a finger, humanity has never lived in such a time where anybody with access to the internet has a colossal amount of options to choose from.

Now, as much as it is useful, what impact does it have on the very way the mind functions or, so to say, the very way the mind has adapted all of its approaches with the options that are available today? Our parents, mostly, married one person and lived their entire lives with them no matter what came their way. They worked it all together. The reason why stability lacks big time in relationships these days is due to the options that are available. All it takes is to move on to the next person.

The mind is designed to divide. And when the mind has a whole world of options in so many forms, what do you think it is going to do? The mind swims in them as if the world is filled with gold and the gold is all its property. The comparison rooted in the mind is not only restricted to relationships but extends to careers, physical appearance, intelligence, wealth, social status, job or career success, education, athletic ability, age, height, weight, fashion sense, popularity, products, relationship status, family background, skills or talents, creativity, moral character, health, life achievements, possessions, influence, beauty, humor, emotional intelligence, resilience, adaptability, cultural knowledge, language proficiency, social media following, academic performance, lifestyle, work ethics, personal hygiene, cooking abilities, travel experiences, and many more.

Look at all the aspects you end up comparing yourself or other people with. Even if you have a loving partner, that doesn't seem to be enough these days, as the world has shown everybody that there are better out there.

The root cause of all human suffering is separation from reality. The mind divides. It is built to divide and find order to keep us humans safe. But is not a reliable tool at all to be seeing reality through its filters.

Work towards living life deeply where there is not a drop of comparison psychologically and only when necessary in the outside world.

~

Lesson 26 — Do not give up on Love.

When we know in the core of our being that this is the person who, for the rest of our life, is meant to be in those memories and beautiful moments that we will remember in the 70s or 80s—do not give up.

Those who give up easily when it comes to love are the ones who:

+ Haven't found *the* person. Not in terms of perfection but *the* one with whom you can be in touch in exactly the same way as you are in touch with your deepest truth. That depth of love is beyond the word or the feeling of love as it arrives—without a start or an end—to be eternally present in that moment of depth. Such a love cannot be fathomed by the hearts and souls of people who haven't seen the depth of life themselves.

+ Have fallen out of love, which was strong at the beginning and over the years has withered away as the two end up living with the images of each other in the mind rather than seeing the person for who they are, here and now.

+ Yes, there are things to be dealt with.

+ Yes, there are pains to be felt or lived.

+ Yes, there will be hard times that will make your blood boil.

+ Yes, the other person and even you will inevitably say or do something that can never be undone, and you have to live with it.

+ Yes, every single person on the planet will face good and bad times in a relationship because it is two different people coming and living together.

Just as on a smaller scale, the atoms release and spend energy, two people coming together will generate a lot of friction, which we word out as problems, conflicts, and incompatibilities.

Here's the thing.

You both, do not have to be fully compatible to be with one another.

The differences in how people are is one of the very reasons that makes the coming together happen in the first place.

Imagine if the first time you met your partner and you both end up having exactly the same qualities and personality that you do have, without an iota of a difference, you wouldn't be able to tell except for appearances who is you and who isn't you. This is not what makes two people fall in love with each other.

We as humankind fall in love—I mean genuine & pure love without corruption—when we see that the other brings in experiences that you by yourself cannot because it is impossible. Just as we see and be with nature and feel good and alive since nature is something outside of us, a partner coming into your life has its own set of unique experiences and limitations too, but on the other hand, has enormous possibilities for growth and change as individuals.

Experiences are the foundation of why we fall in love with another person. If there is depth in the love you share with another.
Do. Not. Give. Up.

~

Lesson 27 — The Choice One Makes.

We all make choices in life. It is the choices we make that define the quality of our life.

+ What we choose to do.

+ Who we choose to be with as a partner.

+ Where we choose to live.

+ How we choose to live.

+ The choice of accepting those few people into our life's circle.

+ The choice of how to be within ourselves.

+ The choice to make changes that help you grow.

+ The choice of leaving a relationship.

+ The choice of the car and the house you buy or live in.

+ The choice of your habits.

+ The choice of wanting to change the old habits that do not serve you anymore.

+ The choice of living in a toxic relationship.

+ The choice of continuing to be in a 9-5 job that we do not like.

+ The choice of respecting your parents.

+ The choice of living a conscious life.

+ The choice of not wanting to know how to live better.

+ The choice of learning something new. The choice of comparing.

+ The choice of living unconsciously.

+ The choice of this juice over the other.

+ The choice of this restaurant over the other.

+ The choice of wearing this pair of clothes.

+ The choice of the pet we get home.
+ The choice of your sexuality.
+ The choice of being committed.
+ The choice of cheating.
+ The choice of not seeing the reality.
+ The choice of being addicted.
+ The choice of what time to wake up.
+ The choice of what to have for breakfast, lunch, and dinner.
+ The choice of whether to go to the gym or do yoga at home.
+ The choice of exercising or not.
+ The choice of taking the bus or the subway,
+ The choice of what to watch and read.
+ The choice of eating a junk meal.
+ The choice of cooking healthy food.
+ The choice of having a child.
+ The choice of getting married.
+ The choice of school, college, university, and what to study.
+ The choice of accepting a job.
+ The choice of shifting career.
+ The choice of going to a doctor.
+ The choice of taking precautions.
+ The choice of living with awareness.
+ The choice of not accepting other's answers but finding out for yourself.
+ The choice of questioning all that life is about.
+ The choice of observing the mind.
+ The choice of looking at life deeply.

+ The choice of believing in the creations of the mind.
+ The choice of following somebody.
+ The choice of forgiving.
+ The choice of letting go.
+ The choice of being empty in the unending moment.
+ The choice of not being aware of one's own body.
+ The choice of reading a book.
+ The choice of facing the pain.
+ The choice of loving.

The only thing in life you do not have a choice about is the death of your body.

Death, too, can be lived with if one can end all their attachments psychologically.

If one can do this moment-to-moment, there will arrive a time when it is possible to be aware and conscious without any choice and that is *the highest form of living where you have no choice but to be aware of the reality*.

~

CHAPTER V — INSIGHT OF YOU.
Lesson 28 — Hurt.

What gets hurt? Is it you? Or is it the personality and images one has built up for decades?

Getting hurt physically is not the same as getting hurt psychologically.

Can you see the mind?

It is not something tangible, but is there. It is the creations of the mind that is getting hurt. When someone says something, what actually is getting hurt is the image of yourself.

What is an image? An image is a capturing of a memory. With all the memories and experiences that you have had, think of all the images turned into personalities that are getting hurt. Those images are as good as dead because they are of the past moments but reflected on in the present by the mind, thus creating time psychologically.

Since one is getting hurt currently, it is obvious that whatever has been stored by the mind is getting hurt, and this includes all the things one has been exposed to in life.

Going forward, is it possible not to record information but to let it pass through?
Be it words, be it moments, be it a person, be it a thing, be it a praise about you, be it an insult too. Nothing needs to be

recorded in order to store it. The mind is brilliant at it already, and this actually frees you up to let the mind do what it does. Just let it pass like a breeze, and nothing will be recorded.

In order to do this, one requires a pure observation that is as sharp as a Swiss army knife. Observing the comments from another and just letting it pass right through you is no joke. Not many people can do this. In such an observation, you are seeing and living the reality of the words itself that is of no significance to reality except in the realms of the human mind.

All the words spoken out loud by you or another person, all the thoughts that you hear, all the memories that you reflect on, all the experiences that you ponder upon—*are not here*. They are a done thing. They do not exist anymore, anywhere in reality except in the mind that is repeating it over and over and over again to keep it alive.

You see, when something is not repeated, it dies out over a period of time. Mind is a perfect, unfathomable machine that is alive in itself, too and wants to be alive as much as you and I want to. It has a life of its own, but it is not separate from reality, just as you aren't. The mind loops everything. The more number of times something has been repeated, the deeper it is in you as a pattern. Some go so deep that you won't even realize they are there but these are what are running in the background, always.

The mind is not against reality at all, but it is because a person is unconscious of what the mind is that propels it to being given such a huge significance, and anything of too much creates an imbalance within the human system.

To restore balance, there needs to be a reality check by yourself of what is real.

What are you? What is this life all about? And if such questions do not yet boil your blood, one must be asking why doesn't it? What is keeping you so busy in day-to-day activities that there is no urge to question the essence of life that is throbbing within your very being? Are the things that are keeping you busy really moving you toward realizing the truth?

The work we do has its place. The words have their place as well. There is no problem if one *chooses* to reflect on their past and any memory but this has to be by choice and not out of compulsion.

One can only get hurt when there is a compulsion with the contents of the mind. It turns out this is a subtle happening that can only come to light with sheer observation. Not superficial observation by the contents of the mind of its own contents, but an observation that is devoid of the mind in that moment of observation. Only then the reality of the mind can be seen where —what and whether you get hurt becomes a choice, too.

~

Lesson 29 — Personalities.

To simply put it—the mind is a machine that copies non-stop.

The so-called personality that we do have is a result of all the behavioral copies of other people. You, by yourself do not have an intrinsic personality of your own, at the deepest level. But the way we behave and are is so deeply engraved that even those who have seen reality cannot escape from having their own personality. The before and after awakening personalities more or less remain, and the only thing that does shift is the perspective.

In today's world, if a person has multiple personalities, he is diagnosed and given a label. If you think about it, how can we even go about in the world and deal with different kinds of people if we do not have the ability to shift our perspectives as and when required? This shift in perspective to deal with things is what invites and requires different approaches.

The problem is not with taking different approaches and different perspectives but with being attached to the identities that come up with the different perspectives.

Lesson 30 — Thoughts.

There are no passing-by thoughts.

You are the one generating it.

You are it when the thinking happens.

You escape from an uncomfortable thought and then sing a song to feel better.

For example, there could be thoughts of arguing with another person in the mind, and after a while there is a song playing all of a sudden. This means the course of thinking in the direction of arguing and anger towards that person and ruminating about an incident has brought about uneasiness, and to avoid facing that for a long time, there is a switch to a song that makes one feel better.

What we connect with in books, movies, or other sources, or even people for that matter, is what we relate and resonate with. What we relate and resonate with is the information that we have gathered throughout our lives, and these become the source of our thinking and the thoughts we generate.

~

Lesson 31 — The Problem of Going Beyond the Mind.

Many spiritual seekers face the challenge of *going beyond the mind.*

The mind, with its constant thoughts, emotions, and judgments, can be a significant obstacle to spiritual growth.

The challenge:

+ The Mind's Nature—The mind is designed to think, analyze, and categorize. It is constantly active, creating a constant stream of thoughts. This constant mental chatter can make it difficult to access deeper levels of consciousness.

+ Attachment—The mind is concerned with self-preservation and desires. It can create resistance to change and grow spiritually, as it fears losing control and identity.

+ Limited Perception—The perception of the mind is limited by its own filters and biases. It can distort reality and prevent us from seeing things as they truly are.

The solution:

The mind has never been the problem. Now, this is something not a lot of people hear in *spirituality*, but there is the root of the problem. I call it "The Paradox of Words."

We require words to live, but the mind has its contents that are deeply embedded with thoughts that are nothing but the words in which we as human beings *think.*

Where thought ends, presence begins.

Lesson 32 — The Paradox of Words in the Quest for Spiritual Enlightenment.

Enlightenment is beyond language.

There are certain words that are widely used in spirituality. An individual may end up connecting to these words in a very deep manner to such an extent that the mind can make them feel they are beyond it. Those very words become a trigger to make them feel more and more enlightened.

This is not enlightenment. Knowledge cannot awaken a person.

Anything out of knowledge cannot be present in that moment of realization. The knowledge one has will still be there to use, but if one makes false meanings out of teachings that were meant for liberation, then that false meaning is what the person ends up living with, thinking they have seen something. Thinking what they have seen cannot be seen by anybody else. Thinking the truth is something to keep it to themselves and not openly talk about and share what they have seen.

It is still the mind attaching itself to those very words that were supposed to give clarity.

This is how complex the mind is.

Unless there is a looking where the contents of the mind do not exist, one cannot be liberated.
They may keep repeating it like a mantra, but it is still the mere words that we humans created and to which the mind grasps onto.

To avoid the already existing dilemmas with spiritual words, I chose the word **Nilness** to express spirituality.

Realization is the most subtlest possibility for a human being. It cannot be achieved or reached or gone after. It is to live *with* the truth and happens only in the absence of the movement of the mind in this very unending moment.

~

Lesson 33 — Distorted Reality.

We look *at* ourselves from the outside a lot of times as if we can *see* the person that we are and then go about living from that view. This is a distorted reality because the only time you do look at yourself is when you have a *reflection* of yourself in a mirror or water or something that reflects *your light* to show how you look and your structure.

Because we have *seen* how we look physically, when we go about living on a day-to-day basis, we tend to *remember* that particular physical appearance and go with it even when there is no reflection. *This* is living with the moment which happened in the past that the mind has stored and clings on to it in the background.

If you had never seen how you look, this distorted background would not have existed. But now that it is unavoidable and you have seen how you are physically, the ability to look at yourself and drop it right after the moment of standing in front of the mirror is equivalent to dropping the distortion. That's all the point of seeing yourself in a mirror is, only at that time.

~

Lesson 34 — Words.

The same words are used in thousands of different ways, and that itself is enough to confuse a person for their entire life, as his understanding of the meaning of those words keeps changing constantly based on what he is being influenced into.

The point is to see that the words are adaptable to our usage, and one needs to come to a stable understanding and differentiation of what the words are used for at their essentiality and when it is being exploited out of context with an intention to influence the readers or listeners.

The meaning of a word each one of us makes is unique to our understanding and application of that word and directly depends on the state of mind we are in and the interpretation we want to give at that moment. Words are subjective to interpretations.

The paradox is that words are the highest form of humanity to express that which cannot be worded out. It is as if an offense against the truth to word it out because it cannot be put into speech. It can only be looked at, perceived, observed, or attended to.

Words are limited, but they also have the power to ignite reflections of oneself to grow and become aware.

Words do not have any meaning by themselves, and yet they are the only way to express humanity. It is the meaning that we, as humans, have given to those words.

Words do have power, but they have no reality outside of the human world. The words are not real in the context of being stuck with them.

This means the words in the human world are strictly limited & adhere to our *speech, writing,* and, above all—*thinking.* There is nowhere else words exist, and however the words are used in the human world, they are *always* going to be interpreted in many different ways since the words are ambiguous in their existence. What one reads and understands is based on their background, personal experiences, and state of mind. When someone else reads the same, they will have their own interpretations, meanings, and significance as the mind of the person who is reading is inclined to a different set of patterns.

Humanity is a culmination of permutations and combinations of the highest order on Earth.

This is why there is randomness and chaos with order in the world.

From one perspective, it all looks fine.
When one looks at the world from other perspectives, there is bound to be bias as to how the world is.

This inherent misconception of framing the world to be this and that is a result of—*randomness with order*. No matter what filter we look at the world through, the *bias is the randomness*, and the *meaning we assign is the order*. We do the same with ourselves and everything in life.

Stay and understand this fact for a while, as these are day-to-day occurrences that not many are aware of.

There is randomness in the mind with all the uncertainties we have in our lives. The mind creates order out of that uncertainty.

The mind creates order out of that uncertainty.

If a person has more uncertainties and a negative frame of mind, the mind has this as its foundation to build on. The danger of this is that the mind ends up creating order out of a negative way of everything. Yes, the person might have good intentions, but *if* the base data for the mind to work with is negative, the order—which is to say the beliefs, the values, the innate qualities of that person, and all that makes them human—gradually becomes chaotic even though for that person it is a way to deal with things and assure themselves everything is alright. Such people, or so to say, such an unconscious mind, *will attract* other unconscious-minded people and *repel* anything that challenges its order.

~

Lesson 35 — Limitation of Words.

Language is all humans have lived with. It has defined the words that a clean-slated child learns, and it is all people talk over and over again. Be it a person far off from a city or someone in a tribe, their language is what ends up defining the majority of who they are. Those languages a person knows are what he can all think about *in*.

Thinking cannot exist without words.

Everybody now has accepted English in most parts of the world. A language made by us with limited letters and a whole dictionary of words that are used in many forms and purposes. But still limited, and each generation keeps repeating the same words throughout their lifetime.

Anything built on that which is limited will always be limited, even if it stands for thousands of years. But seldom do we look at such aspects because the words keep us amused through talking, televisions, movies, theatres, literature, presidents, family, politics, problems, society, songs, history, books, reading, teachings, interpreting, labeling, understanding, inventing, dreaming, consoling, marketing, selling, complaining, discussing, provoking, expanding, and what not.

We named everything we possibly could and continue to do so. This will never stop as well.

What one needs to understand, first intellectually and then the fact of it, is that your name is not *as you* as is not an apple or a tree or the cloud or the stars. It's *our* naming, our word, that identifies the object, but the word is not the object.

One of the problems of the world is we don't even realize this simple fact.

We are full of words, opinions, and interpretations, so much so that there is no space to see that the very words one thinks— *arise*—and they are doing it without being aware of it.

There is so much drive, intention, motive, ambition, and power *with* the words used that it has become too silly to see its birth.

~

Lesson 36 — Understanding the Words.

There are certain words that we grow up with having a negative connotation. This assignment of a negative meaning to certain words and the way another person says it to you could have happened in early childhood due to other people's behavior around us or to us, or it could have seeped in during the experiences we ourselves have had over a period of time.

It is natural to be protective of oneself to avoid getting hurt with similar intentions that we have faced in the past. But it makes a huge difference in being able to differentiate between what genuineness from another person is and *seeing* another person as someone who is attacking us when we look at their actions via a prism of the meanings we have assigned to those words or actions. This is a dilemma that not many people ponder upon even though it exists as brightly in our interactions with other humans as is the air around for us to breathe.

The shift that happens in an instant from feeling good in a conversation with another person to being taken aback is very subtle. But we do feel it with our emotions, and it comes out in the form of anger, repulsion, defensiveness, or ignorance. Now, why does this happen, and where is the root of all this?

There is an imaginary belief that we end up protecting when someone says something that we do not agree with. There is a healthy way of respecting the differences in another person's opinions and his views of the matter. If this is possible to be done by both the people having the conversation, then it is a healthy, genuine conversation where both the people understand and respect where each other comes from, and they do not impose their individual views on the other person by any means.

But usually, what happens is that the meanings we have already assigned to the topic at hand *inhibit* us from totally listening to another person who is sharing their views, as there is constant validation of our own views against theirs. This ends up closing our receiving state of mind which then re-establishes our predetermined beliefs without being open for growth.

There is learning for everybody in how to listen to the words uttered by another person, how to listen to the words that arise in the form of thoughts, and then speak consciously.

All the emotions and turmoils show up as the person is reacting unconsciously.

~

Lesson 37 — The Rise and Fall of Emotions.

The thoughts that you think are solely based on the state that you are in. The state that you are in has everything to do with how the mind has responded to a particular situation, thing, or person.

If you do observe you can clearly see that there is a rush of thoughts when the emotional level is at the peak, be it a positive or negative emotion. For both, the thoughts are being generated by you so rapidly that—for a person who has not seen the mind for what it is—you tend to skip the part that you are the one generating those rapid thoughts because you are experiencing an emotion intensely. The same happens when a person is so involved in a particular activity that they forget who is around and what time it is.

To dive a little deeper.

The rise of emotions:

Emotions are the result of reflecting back on a memory or imagination that picks up on intensity only when you generate thoughts for it. Otherwise, emotions merely pass by like a cloud where you just look at them and do not attach any further meaning or significance.

The fall of emotions:

The emotions do not stay for a long period of time. They are perpetually shifting from one state to the other as the mind flows from one part of the information to the other. How stable you are also shows in the plethora of emotions that arise and fall within you—the time period and the gaps between them. Experiencing emotions is completely normal. But it is the decisions we make when the emotions are high in intensity which is a problem. Because when an emotion is at a peak state it is bound to fall back down. If you make a decision when an emotion is at its peak, there are high chances it's not a conscious decision, and you rethink or regret it when the emotions fall back down. What is called expectation occurs when a decision is made at the peaks of emotions, be it high or low, and then the mind wants to maintain that level involving another person too, which is not the reality but another creation of the mind.

An eerily similar creation of humanity is the stock markets and cryptocurrencies, which are completely based on emotions. It's the emotion of one person trying to bet and match against millions of other people, deciding on their own emotions. Most fail as they aren't stable and patient enough for long term stability and get pulled into the short-term emotional rise and fall.

The stock market and cryptocurrencies are creations and mirrors of human emotions. What we are is projected out into the world in various forms.

You feel the emotions. The emotions are not the words that we have given to them.

Happiness, joy, contentment, satisfaction, pleasure, pride, ecstasy, euphoria, amusement, sadness, grief, sorrow, despair, loneliness, melancholy, depression, anger, irritation, frustration, rage, fury, indignation, annoyance, hostility, fear, anxiety, dread, panic, terror, nervousness, apprehension, worry, surprise, shock, astonishment, amazement, wonder, disgust, revulsion, contempt, loathing, distaste, aversion, affection, fondness, romance, attachment, passion, compassion, infatuation, guilt, regret, remorse, shame, embarrassment, envy, jealousy, covetousness, pride, accomplishment, confidence, hope, optimism, expectation, faith, despair, hopelessness, dejection, contempt, scorn, disdain, gratitude, thankfulness, appreciation, awe, reverence, wonder, respect, boredom, excitement, thrill, enthusiasm, eagerness, relief, comfort, reassurance, satisfaction, fulfillment, contentment, disappointment, letdown, dissatisfaction, confusion, bewilderment, perplexity, curiosity, inquisitiveness, interest, sympathy, empathy, pity, anticipation, expectation, eagerness, indifference, apathy, unconcern, insecurity, uncertainty, self-doubt, nostalgia, longing, reminiscence, annoyance, irritation, love.

All these are mere words.

The words are not the actual feelings of the emotions we experience. Realize this simple fact first.

Actual Emotional Feelings ⇄ Thoughts

The actual feelings rise and fall like the waves of the ocean. They don't stay. If you are aware to see that emotions are one part of this human experience and that there is no need to be attached to them, there will be a great deal of freedom with this realization of the emotion's reality. Not the words but the pure observation of the emotions you feel is itself enough where the mind is nil and the reality of emotions is there for you to see and experience without there being an experiencer. Only then can a person enjoy the emotions without being attached to them. Here is where there is complete freedom.

~

Lesson 38 — Beyond the Grasp of Words and Mind.

The contents of the mind are a hindrance to the truth.

Once you have begun the journey to realize the truth, it depends on the intensity with which you go at it.

Make mistakes, choose the wrong path, follow—only to realize that isn't the way. Do all you are inclined towards and not let yourself be fooled that anybody other than yourself can make you see the truth.

You have to deeply perceive the truth yourself.

To come to such a moment to realize the truth, the contents of the mind cannot exist in that moment of realization. If there is *any* content of the mind, that is still the mind telling you that you have seen something beyond.

That is not the truth. It is yet another subtle way of the mind to be there, even if it feels like *that is it.* You know, there is no *that is it* moment when it comes to awakening.

You just wake up from the unconscious sleep that you have lived in.

To some people, it may happen all at once, and to a lot of other people, it keeps happening. It is just as random as the existence is.

How would you know if you have woken up?

+ When there is no compulsive attachment, not only to the external world of people and things but to the mind as well. That is one of the major ways to ascertain. And this itself is not easy to *do*. It cannot be *done*. There is no *doing* to verify it, too.

+ Another major way is to see how attached you are to the words of the language you think in.

If you truly can see—how other people are attached to the words and how important it is for them to satisfy their mind with the very words they have attached themselves with and go on deepening it with reassurances, that is a clear sign of the mind still keeping up its grasp on the person.

The person may have an inkling that they are over it, but if they are still attached to words, there is work to be done.

~

Lesson 39 — Work.

Work is central to the life that we live, not because of the rewards of it but for us to indulge every day in expressing ourselves. This is why it is best to work on what you love doing without a care for earning out of it.

The majority of the people work for companies or for another person. Many do work by themselves today as individuals. We spend so much time on the work that we do. Take 8-10 hours a day for 5 days a week for 1 year. That's a staggering 2,000+ hours you spend yearly at work, and this is a minimum. But the thing about work is that it does not end when you are off it. The work stays in the mind, and you think about it even when you are not doing the work.

The work shapes you as a person.

What we choose to work on is an essential and the most important decision of our entire life.

If we have picked up a career that we deeply do not enjoy working in and always feel incompetent for it no matter how much we try, that is a clear-cut answer that we are not doing something where we are naturally skilled in.

Figure that out first.

The way the world functions today has messed up our very way of going about what to do in life. We end up asking others and the internet but never ourselves. Even when we do, and there is an answer, the thought of making a life doing that comes about, and we never go back to asking that question again.

Asking questions is the way to go about life.

When we genuinely answer after asking the right questions, we will find that constant questioning brings out great progress within us.

If we do not like a question, that is the question one must reflect more on. The very things we are afraid and fearful about are what we must be doing. That is where our growth is. That is where we will expand ourselves. And in the midst of all this, knowing the reality of the mind is of utmost significance.

We can work because the mind is always functioning in the background. But true creativity also requires a source that is devoid of information. The mind is full of information. The only place without a location that is empty of all matter is **Nilness**. Call it whatever you would want to use the words that exist only in the human ecosystem, but these words will never be that which they describe.

Having an actual realization and diving deeply into the **Nilness** is beyond these words. So when one has the choice of the mind that is awake and a source of **Nilness** that is devoid of knowledge and information or any human creation—a work that lives through centuries can be done. Such a work will not only live through your life but pass right through all the lies and false realities created by the unconscious mind that we see in the world today. This is the power of creations that are born out of the truth.

What you work on takes more than half of your life.

That must hit you like a bullet if you aren't doing what you are really gifted with. Do not let your gifts go to waste. Give them to the world, and you will live a life of giving that is beyond all other contributions that one can make in their lifetime.

If you are like me, who went from job to job, from one country to another, running away from the very thing that I was supposed to do—write—I will tell you one thing: When you sit down to work and have no idea how many hours pass by, *that's the work* you must be doing. It doesn't matter how much it is going to make you now.

Have the courage, jump into this work you know in your being that you are the one for it, and put all your energy into doing this one thing.

When you do this kind of work, the existence aligns with you, too, since you have aligned with your own existence, and there are forces that come together that pave the way for your deep work to shine in the world.

~

Lesson 40 — Do Not Hold Back Your Authenticity.

There is that feeling when you think of showing something to the world, and then you hold back.

You hold back because that is the mind functioning. You hold back:

+ Because the contents of the mind have a conditioning that does not let you go ahead with what you naturally want to do.

+ In that important moment, which could have gone either way, the limitations of the mind come out in full throttle in that subtle moment, does its job reaffirming its already engraved beliefs, and die down momentarily, knowing its unconscious contents were again successful in luring you into acting out of its dead contents.

+ Because you do not know the root of what is holding you back.

+ Thinking what other people would think about the change you were about to make.

All of this, to simply put it—*denies your authenticity*.

+ The authenticity that you yearn for at the 9 to 5 job where it cannot happen because you are contained within the cage of other people's activities of the mind.

+ The authenticity that will make you totally free of functioning at the mercy of other people's rules.

+ The authenticity that *allows* you to fully express and flourish as a human being.

+ The authenticity that lets you begin to see the limitations as well as the beauty of the mind.

+ The authenticity that will make you want to get up in the middle of the night because it is throbbing to come to reality and share it with the world.

+ The authenticity that paves the way for your natural skills and innate qualities to finally come out in full flow.

The very Authenticity that your unfulfilled life has been asking for— to make you whole.

~

Lesson 41 — Find Your Flow.

When one has found what they love doing, there is no effort in how they go about doing what they do. It just *flows*. Make yourself aware that unimaginable things are possible when you *find out that—one thing—you have a passion for, that—thing—that you do when nobody is around, but you really, really like doing it!*

That, my friend, is what you must be truly doing.

When money becomes the foundation for selecting what we do, there is no authenticity in it because we are doing it with an end goal already in sight. This itself limits the scope of how much one can grow in it because the thing about money is that it can make us run behind things that we don't really like doing, but over time, the mind becomes accustomed to it and comes to terms and settles down with what we are doing since it *gets* us the money.

There is no freedom in doing something we do not like. Let's be honest about that for a moment. Just be brutally honest with yourself to see that what you are doing is not aligned with what you really want to do, or else you wouldn't be here spending time reading a book written by somebody else. You would rather spend all your time doing what you really love and not give a hoot about what others are doing because you would be so involved and so focused on doing what you love that you have no time to glance away even a second to something that is not really worth it from what you have deep attention for already. The crux of why I thought of writing this topic is that it is my flow. It is my flow to go on writing and pouring my mind out into the world.

What is your flow in?

If there is any genuine place that has not been explored but you know you must, then the question of "Where is your flow?" must bother you and hit you at the sweet spot since you have not been doing it or paying any attention to it.

107

Why don't you do what you love doing?

If writing is what you really, really want to do, then "Why don't you do it?" Apply anything you want to do with the example of writing that I take here.

Why do you give reasons to not write?

Isn't that what you deeply crave to do and want to turn it into a ticket to get that freedom away from the companies you work for? Ask yourself with utmost honesty and brutality as to why you are not doing the very things that you have the natural and innate skills for? To write in a flow for hours is what writers do best. If you want to be one, then remove all the distractions from your life—personal, professional, and digital.

If you are not precise in what you want to do in life and really care for, it won't manifest in your life. This is a pretty basic understanding. If I don't spend time writing, how can I end up having writing to show for as a result of my writing? If you aren't spending time honing your natural skills, you are going about it all wrong, my friend. You have succumbed to the pressures of the world and the way the world works is that it makes the majority a slave to its way of working.

Get yourself out of the compulsiveness:

+ Get out of the conditionings by first *seeing* that you are a slave to the way the world works.

+ Understand the way the mind works. Read psychology. Read anything and everything you get your hands on that betters and deepens your perception and takes you to higher ground to look at all the problems you have.

+ Make it a moment-to-moment habit to observe your very thoughts. When this is done over a period of time, there are subtle realizations that take you to the root of all the problems you have. It always begins with how the mind has been conditioned ever since you were a child, and this includes all your experiences to date.

Finding what you are most passionate about, which is no different than what is going to drive your purpose in life, can only happen when you eliminate all the other things that you have been spending time on and do not feel genuine about doing those things. This can ironically include the very work that you do and are good at. What you are good at may not always be what you really love doing— which is why it is of utmost importance, to be honest with yourself in order to figure out *what it is that you really have a flow in doing when nobody's watching, there is no money involved in it, but you dance within when you do it.*

Find your flow and you will thank yourself you found it.

~

Lesson 42 — Everybody Reads.

Reading isn't just going over the words of a language. The mind is constantly reading information—Every. Single. Moment.

There is information within you accumulated over the past few decades that is far greater than all that is there on the Internet. Far greater. The contents of the internet are like a drop in front of the contents of the mind.

The information that we do inhabit is something that has framed and conditioned us as an individual. In reality there is no individuality, though to live as a human being and to survive and prosper, we do need a sense of identity. But the conditioning that is set, based on the mountain of information that we inhabit within ourselves, is not easy to observe, and it takes getting through suffering in order to come to a place where one ends up having the *qualities* that allow us to observe these conditionings in the form of stored and outdated information.

The qualities are akin to gold that comes out of all the beatings the ore takes. Life is such that it wants to turn you into gold from the ore. It is not going to stop until one realizes that he is indeed the gold with layers of conditionings that need some dusting.

When you are equipped with the awareness to read these limiting conditionings, you become free of the information that has been thrust upon you.

Reading is the deepest way for a person to *think* in their own voice and absorb the information to the fullest. Writing has been the oldest means of communication for humanity. There is a reason for this, and it has everything to do with the mind.

Content is the main foundation of the internet today, and with most of the content gravitating towards instant gratification, a whole lot of people have lost the sheen of simply writing & reading. This has made them become slaves to technology because they do not *think* with their own voice as to what makes sense and what doesn't but go in the way directed by the advertisements and influences through various media and people.

Reading what has been written makes the reader reflect on themselves in greater depth.

Learning to read the contents of the mind and all of its information by pure observation is a must if one wants to be free of attachments and still use the information when required.

~

Lesson 43 — Share Your Knowledge.

We underestimate our knowledge so much over time that it becomes secondhand, and we don't even realize how much we *do know*. The view of how much we do know gets stunted because we have been doing it for a long time.

What one needs to understand is that there are people out there who are trying to figure out the *A* of it, and here you are knowing *A* to *Z* and everything in between, mostly.

It's time to share your knowledge with the world.

There is no need for it to be perfect.

All you have to be is yourself.

Lesson 44 — Be Humble.

Wherever you go, whoever you meet, be humble.

That is enough to touch anybody's heart.

Humbleness doesn't mean to be inferior. It is an action of simplicity, knowing that there is no inferiority or superiority.

Then, there would be no means to act without being humble.

~

Lesson 45 — Learning.

There is always something to learn and grow in.
You and the smartest person in the world can never know everything because knowing everything is a myth.

+ One cannot know everything, as there is no end to knowing.

+ One may be an expert in a subject and fall flat in day-to-day interactions with loved ones.

+ One may be very intellectual, but they would not know depth as knowledge is limited. They may have immense knowledge, but *depth in living is something that cannot be gained from knowledge but lies outside of it.*

Real learning is when the moment-to-moment experiences come alive with reflections and awareness of the here and now.

Lesson 46 — Dream.

What we dream as we lie asleep is a recycling of all that we have ever experienced in our waking life.

Dreams are not messengers or, as some believe, gods 'way of telling a person what to do. There is no control over what we dream about since the mind is actively trying to retain most of the information that is stored in the form of memories, experiences, and coping mechanisms. The mind tries to retain in ways you cannot imagine.

+ This is the reason why we go on repeating the same things over and over again.

+ This is why, even in waking life, we have patterns. This is why we feel that the same problems occur again and again.

+ This is why we end up with similar partners, where it always ends up miserably.

+ This is why we aren't able to get out of an already existing habit that we know is detrimental to us.

+ This is why we find it so hard to create new habits that serve us for good.

+ This is why there is an instant gratification system in place as the mind repeats in short frames of time for retaining information, though there are also long-term patterns that can span out for decades, too. As information gets lost over a period of time if it is not repeated, the mind hates long-term gratification, which is when a person has to wait to see the results. The mind cannot wait for its information to come forth. It wants to let out random information continuously. Even now, as you read this, if there is no focus or undivided attention, the mind will instantly catch hold of that short time frame to play its recording.

When you are in deep sleep, there is permutation and combination of all your memories at a proportion that you cannot fathom and is impossible in real life. During the day, most people only hear the mind, but as you lay asleep, you are able to actually see the activities of the mind. It looks as if it is real. As if it is happening to you, but the reality is that what you see is the by-product of the already existing memories and emotions.

The emotions, meanings, and interpretations we give to what we already know is an ever-changing process. Dreams, too, are shaped and aligned with our ever-changing perspectives and experiences.

One might have memories that they hold on to dearly—a person or an experience—and this gets tangled up with the emotions and plays out in the most random fashion possible.

Dreaming can even go as deep as though we wake up thinking that it did happen in our real life only to confirm later that it wasn't so.

Although dreams aren't actual physical happenings, they are a way to delve directly into what we need to work on. If one is aware enough of what to make out of a particular dream, it has the potency to take them deep to work out the root causes of many of their problems.

If one reads about what dreams are all about from another person's perspective, then there is no space for the person to find the revelations for themselves by seeing their own dreams. It will hit the hardest when we realize and recognize the interpretations of our dreams. To do this most effectively, one must not function by holding the mind as everything. The mind is just one more aspect that allows us to have such a rich human experience and even go on to question and see what this life is all about.

One must be vulnerable and brutally honest about all aspects of one's life to look at the dreams for what they are and not what one wants them to mean, which is again an activity of the mind trying to assign meanings to the dreams that it itself is responsible for.

To look at a dream for what it is, one must first learn the art of looking at reality for what it is. How one interprets dreams is the same as how one lives and looks at reality in waking life.

If we live consciously, being aware of all that is happening and all that we do, and seeing the mind for what it is, we will do the same to the stories we dream of, too.

~

Lesson 47 — Long-Term Gratification.

There is something about not falling for the short-term instant gratifications.

When you have the patience to wait, it is a gift that many do not possess. It is only over time that you can look back at something to see how much you have grown. When you are 30 and look back, only because there is a long-term to look at can you have a significant reflection on the life that you have lived. This is reflecting on your memories that are of the past.

There is a common phrase, "Give it some time." We all somehow know that with time, there will be results. But how many have the patience to wait and keep doing what they do without expecting anything out of it?

It is in that time period when you do not force something to happen that takes you to a place where it does happen.

When you want something really badly and instantly, you may get it, but that is the mind wanting a fix. There is no fulfillment in drinking, succumbing to the desires that arise out of compulsiveness. But there is definitely fulfillment and satisfaction when you have worked on something for a duration of years and kept it going. It is the same reason why there is a sense of accomplishment after earning a degree after studying for two, four, or ten years. You celebrate the long-term investment that you have made.

Where does the short-term gratification come in? From the compulsive mind that you are not aware of. From the mind that has been running on its own from the moment it started, and there was nobody to look after it. It is like a kid who was never taught anything and always did whatever he wanted to. Wouldn't this kid grow up to live a life where he wouldn't know the difference between what to do and what not to do?

If you have never looked at the contents of the mind that dictates each second of your life, it is the compulsive mind that is looking for short-term gratification. It wants to keep watching the videos and the movies endlessly because they are easy to do.

The compulsive mind will and can only do what is easy.

It doesn't want to work for something long-term that requires consistent work for years—be it with a partner, with the work you do, or with yourself for your own growth.

The mind that you become conscious of will only work towards the long-term of nearly everything, leaving out the day-to-day stuff. Be it relationships, work, or life.

The reality has no time. When you, too, see the timelessness of reality, all the short-term approaches fall off, paving the way for the mind to align with the timeless reality where there can be nothing but long-term approaches.

~

Lesson 48 — Reality.

Enlightenment or liberation is not something that can be thought, spoken, or expressed without corrupting what it actually is. Words that we use in various languages are for understanding. An understanding with *only* those that belong to our species. That's all the words are for. This is very hard for a lot of people to live with. Not just read and say yes and still look at it the same way. Words are important since speaking is how we share and communicate with other people of our clan.

But merely understanding intellectually that words are mere words and not living that life, where one is not even attached to words, makes a hell of a difference. This is the difference between one who *can* see reality and one who is totally absorbed and lives in the illusory world the mind has created. I lay immense emphasis on this because what you *think* are words of your own language.

Thoughts are one of the prevalent and dominating parts of the human mind; the other is our imagination, which is still in the realm of memories. Memory is built from the past and becomes an ingrained memory when it has been repeated in a loop a lot of times. Over a period of time, only the strongest memory sticks for remembering, but even these are not reliable as time changes the retention of the actual moments over a period.

Again, memory is of the past, and imagination is of those memories mixed with the future, creating a permutation based on the individual's personality, way of thinking, and patterns. *All* this still occurs in the present unending moment, the only difference being the individual is not aware of the reality of this unending moment but rather in a world created by the mind over the course of their lifetime.

When one comes to a point where they can see that words are the thoughts they think over and over again, see the limitation of their language vocabulary, and the limitation of all the language vocabulary that humans have created for their own sake, then and only then can a person see the reality without corrupting it with the happenings of the mind.

In spirituality, often thoughts, thinking, and mind are spoken about a lot. But if one can observe, really observe, that the *crux* of thinking is words and is willing to go beyond the words, it is possible for them to *look* and *live* in reality.

+ A reality that is just there.

+ A reality that does not need to be interpreted or made meanings out of.

+ A reality that *is* the present unending moment.

+ A reality that is beautifully knitted with millions of different flavors of life with an unfiltered view.

+ A reality that is free of not only the outside influences but also of the influences of one's own powerful but limited mind.

~

Lesson 49 — Limited Energy.

We cannot keep responding to all the stimuli we encounter.

There is a limited amount of energy, physically and mentally, which depends on a lot of factors.

Attuning to these factors for ourselves, being aware of the specific scenarios where energy is spent or drained out takes the person a long way in understanding, switching back the control to their hands, and re-routing their energy right from the start of the day to something that they truly value.

If not done, the habits of a day turn into years pretty quickly, leaving you spread out all over the place.

~

Lesson 50 — Nilness as Foundation.

What comes to you naturally is what your strength really is. What is acquired through learning and gathering knowledge should ideally be aiding to enhance those natural strengths but that is not how the world or people are going about it. There are aspects we come to realize we are not good with. No matter how much you try, they just don't seem to come naturally to you. The majority of us force ourselves to get good at our weak points keeping the end results of making money or to get along with other people. Even if it works out, it can only be short-lived because one has started from the point that they lacked something and went on to fill that void in pursuit of something. Such pursuits that are not based on truth will always be short-lived as the foundation itself is not based on what one knows but on what one doesn't know.

This is hard to understand intellectually if one is fixated on beliefs and ideas, which are the most dangerous barriers to seeing what everything really is about. But if one has come to a point in their life where they have realized their self-held beliefs and ideas about—themselves, their family, their friends, society, the world, and life itself—are nothing but dramas that are inflicted on us during childhood, sustained as we grow up, and we hold on to those dramas and create new one's based on old dramas. This could sound really blunt to a lot of people, but it is a fact that majority of the humankind does not want to or is not equipped to look into it. For those whose survival is a challenge on a day-to-day basis, it is understandable that it doesn't make sense for them to think of anything beyond working for their daily bread. But those who have the basic necessities of living do not have any valid reason to not look into this matter of how and what is really driving their actions and thinking, day in and day out.

Allow me to share a small story.

A baby is born, and he or she comes into this world, and we say, "Welcome to the world, little one!" He opens his eyes for the very first time and looks at the people and everything else hazily. As time goes by, the vision gets clearer, and all the sounds repeated to the baby start falling into a certain pattern of the language those people around are speaking. Then, the baby starts to notice the reactions of people when he blabbers something or smiles, invoking a sense of joy in others, which in turn becomes a reflex action, and the baby continues to learn based on the people around. His learning has a *foundation—in* the nature of the people around him. If a child was born and kept away from interacting with humans, he wouldn't know of language and all the words that come with it. A child that is brought up being trained with a particular language and culture he is born into, becomes that. There is no denying this fact. What is more important to understand here is the state of understanding and perception that the people around the child are in while he is brought up. This ends up being the most vital aspect of the child's mental framework. Just to see that this has been their foundation takes decades for a lot of people and most don't even realize the influences others have had on them. This is where all of our beliefs and ideas come from. Add to it the thousand different ways we are exposed to information now which makes it even harder to distinguish between the influences and the facts.

Assuming you are a healthy human with the gifts of seeing with both your eyes, listening with your two ears, breathing and smelling with your nose, eating and drinking with your mouth, and feeling with your skin. What we are trained from childhood is to see, hear, and identify whatever one smells, tastes, and touches.

+ *Nobody.* Nobody shows the physical space that is there between your body and the object or person that you see.

+ Nobody tells us all that we hear is sound in various forms, including our *subtle thinking*.

+ Nobody talks about the magic of breath that we do, and we do not have control over at the same time.

+ Nobody tells us about the beauty of tasting food that nurtures the body.

+ Nobody knows the art of listening, the art of sensing without interpretation.

+ *Nobody teaches us to human without the influences of being human. That is where the truth of life lies. To be human and not to be at any moment.*

When this state of **Nilness** becomes a *foundation*, any pursuit built on top of this is ever-lasting and not short-lived.

What you really are begins to express itself without any effort because the actions are then coming out of the truth of your existence which is a fact and not out of imagination and memories.

~

CHAPTER VI — THE ART OF ELIMINATING.

A distraction-free approach is a must in today's world. The internet has a lot of potential, but it also has a hell of a lot of distractions. How can one be focused on writing when one is all over the place, with multiple social media accounts open in other tabs and peeping into what others are doing?

Social media and the internet can either be a boon and a ticket to freedom from everything that holds you back, or they can become a fish marketplace where you only look and buy rotten fish based on what others do on the internet.

Growing is the most essential need of a human being. If you are using the internet and all that it offers to grow day after day into something you stop recognizing month after month or even week after week, that's the way to do it.

I was all over the place, even though I used to think of myself as a minimalist. But the paradox of life is such that there is always room to grow in each and everything about you on a day-to-day basis. Narrow down what you really want to do in life and start doing it. By doing so, you will find that satisfaction comes not only daily but also from living with a purpose and waking up to it with the life force of creation backing you up.

Let's face it. We use a laptop or a computer because we have a *lot* of data to work with. The field in which we work only makes it more complicated to keep everything organized. Unless you are a person who keeps everything clean and tidy, which is very few of us, the laptop is bound to be full of scattered files.

Do the hard job of going through every file you have and delete those that are not worthwhile to take up space on the machine you use daily. Be aware that this is also a machine that you expose the mind to, and the mind is such that it will soak in each and everything—even a glance. Though you may not remember it, the mind does and swings you back to something else while you are working.

This habit takes time to master but is essential to getting rid of all the things that no longer serve you. It will keep you up at night because it is there.

There is tremendous freedom in removing all that is not in the present. Very few people deeply get this, but we hold on to the past items to keep them alive physically, even though we believe we have moved on from them. The mind itself is a complex machinery that does everything to not be here in the now, which is essentially where you will sit to write and do all the work you do and which is the only place to be.

There's freedom in eliminating. The past and the future are only of the mind.

I steer into the mind here because the mind is at the core of distractions. The mind itself is not a distraction, but its repetitiveness is. When something plays on a loop for a long time, there is no room for freshness or new insights. Hence, being in the contents of the mind is the primary elimination that one needs first to observe and navigate while writing.

Take back charge of the mind just like you would with the steering wheel when the car goes off route.

The way to do this efficiently is to first see in that instant that the mind has gone into repeating and reaffirming one of its old patterns and then take charge by turning the content on its head with something you are good at.

One needs to cultivate and test the methods that work best for them. What someone else would give you will not work to eliminate the pattern. When *you* find out the ways by yourself by reiterating what makes you take back the charge of the mind when it goes on a repeating state, *that* is what will work for you to *eliminate* the mental pattern that is unique to you based on your personal experiences.

Not at once, but once the new healthy patterns of eliminating old unaided ones are established, it becomes a moment-to-moment realization of all that the mind does to keep you in its patterns.

Dive into the root of the *thought* that came up while you started reading this. Yes, that one.

Look at the words that do come up and the meanings assigned to them in the background. As you carefully observe and see, whenever a thought comes up unconsciously, you will be able to *hold* it at the very instance it happens and *look* at it as if you are holding something in your hands, the difference being that you do not have it physically but mentally.
Holding thoughts and their occurrence the moment they occur is the highest form of eliminating what the mind is doing.

Lesson 51 — The Journey.

There are no fixed step by step approach people can take to heal themselves emotionally.

Emotions are what make us connect and experience. When past experiences affect our emotions, and we end up developing unhealthy coping mechanisms, it is difficult to see these ourselves. Emotions are varied and unique to the person based on their specific scenarios and experiences.

There are emotions involved with spirituality, too, and the strongest is when one thinks of their spiritual journey.

There is no need to get confused about the word *journey* when it comes to spirituality.

Yes, one does not need to go anywhere to realize and be aware. Yes, there is no journey to be in this present unending moment.

But *there is a journey* that is ushered at a certain point, which marks a drastic *shift* in the way a person looks at life itself. That shift will change their view completely and irrevocably.

There is no way back to their previous perspective, as it has now risen to a different depth. This is how it is. Once a person begins to see and work towards not material freedom but inner freedom, *inner freedom begets all other human freedom*. It makes us do more and more internal work as it brings about a total change, and the person knows it deep within themselves that this is the way.

Now, the initial revelations could happen with all the approaches out there, but many of them have intentions of leading you somewhere. That is not a freeway but a controlled environment with the intent or dream of a person or an organization. There is no freedom in attaining that which is already set for you by another human.

The truth cannot be attained as it is something that is not attainable.

Somebody can spend years and decades following and end up nowhere or realizing it was all a waste since the path itself had a destination, and when they reach that point, they still feel lost, in a different way than when they found it the first time but still lost.

That is why there is a journey. Nobody gets it right the first time. Not even Buddha did. Everyone has to go through a journey as the revelations keep coming to the person in a thousand different ways. To make *sense* of it all—takes time.

Not all the problems can be solved at once. In the same way, *not all the blocks that prevent one from seeing the reality or the truth can be eliminated at once. It is an ongoing, progressive work.* But what people end up doing mostly is getting hooked to the short pleasures of the mind projecting itself as the truth in a million different ways. This is pretty challenging to distinguish if one is caught up with their thinking and not even knowing that it is an activity of the mind.

During meditation, one might become content with their own thoughts and the sights they see. Meditation is not that. Meditation has nothing to do with action of any sort, mentally or physically.

Pure meditation is one that lets you see—not with your eyes or the mind—that there is no separation between any damn thing. Not even you and the space around you. This is difficult to *think* about as the mind cannot grasp that which is beyond its nature of dividing.

Pure meditation is to become aware of who you are, which is the unmoved mover. That which is *eternally still*—has and will never move—but that which moves everything in existence. That which is in the entirety of all reality.

To arrive to see this without a start or end takes a human being on a journey filled with revelations about himself, the rest of humanity, and reality.

The journey from a human point of view involves immense growth as a person in what they have known till now and taking the leap of faith into the unknown as they continue working on eliminating all that is holding them back.

~

Lesson 52 — Revelations.

Flashes of images, thoughts, feelings, and memories have the potency of taking the conscious mind to the root of a person's current action.

A reflection always involves the mind as it is the mind where the memories are contained.

Revelations happen when you reflect. This reflection is of the past as it involves memories and experiences. A reflection—though it happens in this unending moment—you, as this consciousness being fully aware that you are doing so, dive into the contents of the mind to make sense of something that will aid you in eliminating a pattern of the mind when you see it as clear as reality.

This includes everything a person does and the way he lives.

For example:

Say your partner is sleeping in the bedroom, and you do not want to disturb them. You are quite okay with getting ready after a shower in the hall with minimal light.

In the midst of all this, you get a flash of a memory spent with your parents on one of the trips—Revelation.

You hold onto this flashback for a while as you get ready, and it suddenly dawns on you that the memory that popped up at that instant of choosing to respect and not disturb the sleeping partner is indeed coming from the choices that your parents made and lived by during your childhood.

Revelations take us back to the source of where our current actions, behaviors, thinking, habits, and patterns come from.

Such revelations may seem tiny, but they are not.

When this awareness of what the unconscious mind is choosing to do in the present moment is linked with the root of where it is coming from, the pattern recognition of the choices that do not serve us anymore and seeing the root of it itself leads to the dissolving of the negative patterns.

Such revelations in the form of flashbacks in our memory happen all the time. All you have to do is be aware and observe as they come in order to see the connection between what you are doing or thinking currently and the root of where it is coming from—that is, the flashback you just became aware of.

~

Lesson 53 — Save Yourself from Yourself.

I am not here to save anybody.
You have to save yourself from yourself.
There is no other danger psychologically.

It is time to accept that we now have the resources at hand to work out *all* that we have been doing *compulsively*, and that includes compulsive thinking, too.

To take this as a responsibility is the most responsible thing one will ever do for oneself to begin this journey of lifelong contentment, long-lasting peace, and clarity.

The most I can do as a person imparting conscious writing is be by your side while you work out the unconscious contents from the system.

Till now, there has only been an accumulation of unconscious contents and living unconsciously.

The elimination and awareness of unconsciousness is itself consciousness.

Though the elimination of unconscious contents is a gradual process, there are major chunks in the form of beliefs that pave the way for consciousness when these chunks are looked at with complete attention without escaping from it.

~

Lesson 54 — Flow of Life.

There is nothing that can actually be controlled. It is all a flow.

If one gets caught up and tries to hold the flow of life, there will be misery.

When a person is not in sync with the ever-flowing stream of existence and believes they can change the flow according to their limited sense of understanding, they end up going in the opposite direction of the flow and suffer. That is not the way it works.

An individual who can clearly look without being perturbed by the various happenings around and inside them will see that the tide of life flows in the most random way but is never in turmoil as there is ordered randomness.

The human mind cannot come to terms with this as it has been ordained time after time to follow and survive, which makes one stand their ground and not ease into the flow of life itself. The survival mode of the mind resists the flow of life.

Once a person realizes the fact that there is no point in being against the flow, one can learn to turn around and come to a simple place to let the flow do its thing while you enjoy its ride. This doesn't meant to just sit and do nothing but to allow oneself to sync back to the flow in relation to oneself and everything else. The allowing for this is effortless—only then can one make efforts in the outside world along with being utterly free of the results or consequences.

At this point, because there is no attachment to what one is doing or receiving, and as one is conscious of the way of the flow, there comes freedom in not living against it and letting go of controlling what has never been graspable in the first place.

~

Lesson 55 — Ending = Death.

When you can let the thoughts that make you suffer pass through, just as the breeze touches and passes over, in that moment of awareness, there is an ending from it.

It all ends in a matter of a few seconds. Not even minutes. All that you have built will come to an end. This is the reality of life. This is what people are deeply afraid of. This is why there is fear in many different ways, but the fact is that—it is the not knowing about death.

How can one know death if they cannot be alive afterward to know it? Knowing happens when one is alive and has a memory of things. Death is literally the end of all of it. So you see, it is impossible to *know* death. One is comfortable with what they know so that they can dance and swim in the world with that knowledge and survive. Death, or as I like to call it—ending—is unknown and will always remain unknown because it cannot be known logically with our petty little brains. One has to perceive death beyond this biological entity.

As human beings, what one *can* do to not be afraid of death is by getting comfortable with *ending*, no matter what it is.

End your ego. End your fears. End unhealthy people from your life. End psychological patterns.

End all that is possible psychologically, and then there will be no fear of ending, which is no different from death, which is no different from being alive.

The problem with everyone is they do not end something completely. They keep it around to get back when necessary. Be it a memory, an experience, or anything that comes out of their psychological knowledge.

When you want to think positively, the mind thinks positive thoughts. When you want to think negatively, the mind thinks negative thoughts. It goes where you *direct* it.

So the next logical question that the mind would ask is, "How can I direct my mind to end itself?" You see, it is *still* the mind asking that question, and this is the paradox of life. One cannot end the mind because we will be dead without it. The notion of ending the mind is a complete joke. The solution for this needs to come by *looking* at what the mind is doing first. Then, with that very attention, the activity of the mind stops, which shows the fact that when a human being looks at the mind.. are you with me? I will repeat this:

When a human being looks at the mind, the activity of thoughts ceases.

It may stop instantly or gradually depending on the degree of attention that is lit upon the thoughts, which is thinking, which is, in turn, an activity of the mind. Anybody who is sensitive enough to give this a try will see that this *does happen*. Now, one may wonder why would the thoughts stop when you simply look at it? It stops because the true authoritarian has become aware of *what* the petty mind is doing or, so to say—what the true authoritarian has allowed the mind *all this while* to let it do whatever it wants unconsciously. It has wandered all over the place. When you become aware, or you become conscious, or *that* which is the creator wakes up from a deep sleep to see what its creation has been doing, that is when you can *look* at the mind to see what it has been doing *all this while* as you have been unaware. When you become observant and simply look, the *subtle* nature of the mind and the *subtle* nature of who you are become one. *Paying attention to thoughts simply makes it nil, and that is when a stillness arrives that is devoid of any corruption.*
A stillness where the thoughts stop existing for a while or a stillness where the thoughts are thought out consciously is a gateway to **Nilness**. Here, there is space that allows you to actually *be* in unity with the rest of humanity and existence. That is the power this kind of stillness has in **Nilness**.

The mind is *yours* to take charge of to route, re-route, and direct it wherever you wish to go. In one way, it has no existence without you.

The mind exists because you exist. What you listen to as thoughts is what *you* are *thinking*. There is no difference at all. It is *you* who uses the mind when you want it, but it is not separate from you, and at the same time, you are not the unconscious mind that goes on endlessly because such an unaware mind exists in time with past and future. But when I say the mind is not separate from you, that is when you are allowing the birth of thoughts when you want it, consciously. This need not happen all the time, but when you become more and more aware, there is no difference in the existence of the mind and you, as you are present and aware of all of its contents.

What the phrase *end of suffering* really signifies is the dissolution of the mind. Because the mind is the reason why there is suffering in the first place but the paradox is that the mind is not the problem. When I mention the mind in a negative connotation, it is only in the context of those people who are living in the contents of the mind, which is when the mind is the problem. It is similar to when you live in your house and think that it is the world. All you are doing is fooling yourself because there is an entire world out there.

Mind is the house you are living in, but there is a deeper way to experience and live a life where the mind falls into its proper place and the time that the mind creates psychologically ends, too. Only then can death and life *be lived as one* in this unending, timeless reality.

~

CHAPTER VII — BEYOND HUMANITY.

Lesson 56 — You are the Universe.

There are things in nature that we don't get bored of even after watching it so many times. This is because—what you see and what you are in those moments are not different at all.

We run on experiences. But it comes with a cost. One experiences and keeps experiencing their entire life in millions of different ways. But there is an inherent cost of being in these experiences that doesn't let the person see the realities other than their self-created world.

It takes a complete shift of what you as a human are now. It is a moment-to-moment actualization of the truth. Actually living it as a human, not by experiencing such a reality but really living it.

There is a passing by, that is void of everything, and a human being can be that void by choosing to live that way. Not by becoming something and taking it as yet another identity but by being free of all identities that arise from all the becomings.

We, tiny humans, are not even a speck in this scale of the universe. It is as if won't make any difference if we stop to exist this very moment. At the same time we are not different than the entire universe.

~

Lesson 57 — It Always Comes Around.

Call it karma or any word you want to. What keeps coming back in your life is not the word itself but a result of the repetitive way one lives.

Each and every word that you speak and think is all about yourself. There is no selfishness in this or selflessness. It is a reality that it cannot be about anybody or anything else because it is all a making of the mind that has been shaped by you.

The same things keep repeating in life since the mind is repetitive. When you are caught in a loop, there is not much growth or progress as a human being. You just go on circling in the loop itself. There is nothing outside of the loop that you see or experience. There is a tremendous limitation in this constricted way of living.

Life is not limited. The flow of life is not constricted but instead is the opposite. It is a flow.

To step out of the loop, one needs to first see the loop that they are in. First, see that it is the mind that is always on a repeat, which puts our life experiences on a repeat.

The mind is an energy form that is common to all humanity. This energy attracts other energies that are alike it. If you are not conscious of the mind and all of its activities, you will keep living in the loop and attracting people and situations that reciprocate the state of the mind.

The way to break out of this loop of the repetitive mind is to see the mind for what it is.

Observe the thoughts, and you will come to realize that the thoughts do not happen on their own—you are the one producing each and every thought and all the happenings in the mind.

That there is no difference between the sound of the thought and the sound that you hear in the outside world.

One is so caught up in the contents of the mind that there is no space to see the reality of the mind. Once you see the reality of the mind, all the baggage of memory becomes light since you do not carry it anymore. They are just there to be used whenever you want to.

Learning from the repetitive situations in life and getting to the root cause of it that has arisen out of the mind ends the loop we have been living in and shows us a different world that we have been completely blind to.

This new world is not at all different physically. But, it is a totally different depth of perception in your little human experiences. After this, nothing comes around and even if it does, that leads you deeper and deeper.

~

Lesson 58 — Numbers.

Numbers are illusions. Numbers are makings of humanity. They did not fall from the sky. Numbers are a creation of the mind.

Now, think of how much you are already invested in daily life with numbers.

Time, measurements, money, savings, investments, internet, computing, counting, phone numbers, addresses, economy, science, technology, games, music, records, education, calendars, business, finance, marketing, age, and health—all have numbers, and they cease to make sense if numbers are taken out.

The numbers are what we created for our usefulness. It has no reality to it outside the human world. Now, if something does not have an existence outside of human understanding, how can that be universal? Numbers can be called global because we are spread out globally across the planet, but they cannot be called universal since they don't exist where humans do not exist or have not entered.

Numbers are, of course, necessary for our daily lives. But that is it.

We don't need to be so indulged in the numbers where we happen to live without being able to differentiate their usefulness from reality.

Consider that you have watched a video or a picture of the galaxies out there as depicted by scientific studies. Now, no man has ever seen that with their eyes, and no man can ever see it the way the telescopes capture such structures. The fact in this is that we are looking *through* the creation of what we have built as humans since there is curiosity to know more and more. But these very images and the movies that we end up creating and watching *severely obstruct* the view of reality that is right here. Even if a person attempts to be in this unending moment

—because of the very reason that he has already seen and been baffled by the images of such beauty and splendor—he ends up connecting what he *assumes* is the reality by imagining those images which is still the content of the mind.

The true reality is perceived when there is not even an iota of the contents of the mind in *that* moment of looking—be it within or on the outside, as there is no difference whatsoever.

~

Lesson 59 — Insight on Existence.

An individual goes through a low phase in their life when something is taken away from them.

Death of someone dear, loss of a relationship, or be it a financial crisis—there was something, and then there is a lack of it.

That period of experiencing a void seems unbearable because there is a sudden shift from *being something* in relation to something or someone *to* not *being that*.

In hindsight, there is a feeling of having grown out of that low phase or moved on from it since the beginning of the growth out of the void arises with **Nilness**. Growth as a human being begins from a point of suffering that takes one to the void of **Nilness**. If one is fully aware of the **Nilness**, such a seemingly low phase cannot affect one's state of being. It will have no power over the person because each moment is a passing by.

A human *being* is an *existing* state.

A human being who masters **The Art of Nilness** *is in a state of existing and not existing by choice.*

Lesson 60 — Time.

Time, living, and dying are not different. This world, this physical reality as we know it, has come into existence out of nothing.

In exactly the same way you started existing even before your physical birth—in exactly the same way there is silence that we hear, and then there is not—in exactly the same way the *thoughts* rise and fall into something that doesn't seemingly exist.

That state of nothing cannot be proved because it encompasses everything in this universe, from the enormous galaxies to the depths of the silence in the human mind.

It is here and not here at the same instant.

Not a single thing can exist without it.

What we see is the results from it. It itself cannot be seen with these petty little naked eyes. But what this organism is capable of is using the gift of perception to witness the wonder and the dream of it all—till he can.

Can you see the beauty of it?

The illusion of time:

There is a vague estimate that out of 8.2 billion, only 820 people can be considered to be enlightened.

That makes it 0.0000001% of the few people who have seen the illusions of the mind, did the work to see the reality, and be free of the compulsive mind.
The rest 99.9999999% of the population, live in the illusions of the mind, did not do the work, and are not free of the compulsive mind.

At the crux of the illusions and compulsiveness of the mind is time.
Time is the one entity we all are running around, yet we never

come to terms with the fact that it is a creation of the mind.

What is time?

Could it be that the 24 hours we live in is entirely psychological? Could it be that the memories we think of and the future we plan for are entirely psychological? We need the clock to function and go about our daily activities. However, one also needs clarity regarding time. Or is there time at all, psychologically?

Time is memory since the mind requires information to make meaning. The mind can only function with information. If there were no information at all, a person would be free of the human mind. This is what enlightenment or awakening is all about in that moment.

In that minutest moment of awakening or enlightenment, the person's mind is not functioning, meaning the person has seen the other way of being, which is possible for each human being— to be in this unending moment without the content of the mind.

The mind has never been a problem.
The time created by the mind has never been a problem.
Living in that creation of the mind, in its contents, is the actual problem.

I have 1 hour to get ready. I have 30 minutes. The meeting will be at 10 AM. Let's meet at 6 PM. I have 1 year to live. I have 50 years to live. This is our 25th anniversary. He was born on 3rd January. 29th February comes once in four years. There are 364 days in a year. I went to Australia 20 years ago. I will complete this by tomorrow. I wish I knew this in my 20s. This movie is for 3 hours. The article is a 5-minute read. That song runs for 10 minutes. It takes 2 hours on the subway. The flight takes 3 hours. All of these and millions of other phrases we use are mere words, and time is deeply sustained in them in the form of past and future, which is a creation of the mind.

You are a timeless being.
But the mind that you possess can only be in time.

Here is what you must become aware of to live in a reality that is timeless, eternal, and unending.

~

Lesson 61 — There Is No Reincarnation.

This moment is all there ever was, there ever is, and ever will be.

The mind has created concepts to keep a person hooked to a future where he will be born again. It is all but a postponement to *look* at what is there now. Because the person does not want to or have the capacity or the courage to look at all the things that are in conflict in this very lifespan, the mind puts reincarnation as the cushion on which a person can sleep over all the things he must work on, but doesn't.

Reincarnation is a belief that has been instilled in the mind through repeated stories over and over again. It is not the truth.

There is only this unending moment, which is hard to describe in words. It is rather a flow of existence where there is no separation.

+ Where your thoughts and reality are not separate.

+ Where the mind and the rest of existence can live in harmony.

+ Where there is no illusion of compulsive *thinking*.

+ Where there is oneness of existence.

+ Where there is no division of any sort.

+ Where time does not exist psychologically.

+ Where the self has dissolved.

+ Where there is a deep flowing perception beyond the senses that is along with reality.

+ Where seeing, breathing, listening, acting, talking, and thinking—all happen instantly, right here and right now. It is as if we are moving along with the rest of existence, but there is no movement at all. There is immense beauty in realizing this.

+ Where the conceptualizing mind ends.

+ Where *at the end of each and every thought, there is a possibility of enlightenment.*

The only way non-duality can come into one's perception is by *observing intensely without any effort.*

~

Lesson 62 — Reality is Timeless.

If one is not aware of what the mind is, there is no way of having peace of mind.

The quest to attain peace of mind, being in the mind, for the lack of better words—is a piece of trash. It is equivalent to swimming in the water but wanting to breathe. It is impossible. One has to go beyond the water to breathe naturally as a human being. In the same way, one has to go beyond the mind to *see* what the mind is and all that it does to a person. How it controls each and everything we do, think, act, behave, decide, and experience.

Now, when one is completely occupied in the contents of the mind, all that can be done is *of* the mind. Whatever we have as a storage in the mind is what we are going to act out of. This is no theory but is as practical and plain as the sky and the water. The problem is that we do not and cannot see these simple facts as there is deep involvement with the contents of the mind.

How can one see this activity of the mind? There is a way that doesn't involve the mind.

+ Observation.

+ Looking.

+ Seeing.

+ Attention.

Call it what you want. The words do not matter because, in that looking, there are no words, and it also signifies there is no content of the mind. The mind can still play its tricks to get back to its contents, but *when there is a conscious looking, the mind cannot exist. This is the truth.*

The mind cannot exist with the reality.

But to live in this world, one can come to *an attainment that allows the mind to be symbiotic with reality. This takes enormous inner work.* It is not easy. If we think the work in the external world is challenging and energy-consuming, give inner work a try. The energy required to handle external aspects is nothing in front of the attention required to *see* and to *observe* the activity of the mind that is constantly in action right from the moment we were fertilized. To see the activity of the mind that has soaked in each and everything—the very unconscious mind that you live with every moment right now as you sit there and read this.

Being free of the mind and being able to use it when we want it confuses a lot of people.
The confusion itself is of the mind.
Do you see that?

Only the mind can be confused and not the reality. Reality is just there. It doesn't even require our attention as we are the one missing out on being in sync with it and not the other way around. But as a human being, to go as deep as perceiving **Nilness** and be able to live with it on a day-to-day basis is something the mind cannot grasp as it involves reality. Where there is reality, the mind does not have anything to hold on to and loses its grip on its contents to make you stay in its time that doesn't exist in reality.

Reality is timeless.

You, when you are in this unending moment, there is an essence of timelessness that comes into your humanity.

Such a perception that is not of the mind cannot be verbalized with what the mind holds dear. There is **Nilness** that comes into the perception of the biological human that we are. This deep combination of being able to *be with the truth* is the dance of spirituality.

When I say dance, it is the conscious awareness of the reality, the truth, and in that instance of awareness, you are the whole of humanity, the whole of existence, and this takes place only because there is a perception of **Nilness** as a human being.

Where you can see and live in the world without time.

Lesson 63 — Spiritual Awakening Through Sound.

One can harness the power of soundscapes to transform the inner world. Sound is an entity of life in the human world that cannot be escaped from. Not a single human being with intact hearing ability can run away from sound. Sound is the very essence of human life and existence itself.

+ Without sound, there would be no movement.

+ Without sound, there would be no creation.

+ Without sound, there would be no nature.

+ Without sound, there would be no music.

+ Without sound, there would be no words.

+ *Without sound, there would be no thoughts.*

The last part is of immense significance if one gets to the depths of it. Thinking at its core is a sound—a sound not on the outside but within the realm of the mind. This doesn't mean the mind differs from existence or human life. It is all one happening.

But to first understand the nature of the mind, one needs to observe its reality, pay attention to thoughts, reflect on actions and behaviors, and perceive all the senses of one's body. The whole sensation of the body can only be experienced when one is completely *with* the body. To be with the body, one needs to see that it is the only means one has to experience life.

The body is a medium to perceive the creation. We are aware that the body has senses of:

+ Touch.

+ Hearing.

+ Sight.

+ Smell.

+ Taste.

All these are not separate occurrences. From the micro happenings of a single cell to the movement of the body to the level of thinking, all this is happening in unison. These are not individual occurrences, as it may seem when one goes about understanding through the mind's contents.

The mind is designed to break things up. It is designed to split and separate everything, lay it on the table, and pick the best possible solution for any given situation or problem. It is of use when it comes to certain things in the world but not in terms of looking at reality as it is. All the senses of your body occur simultaneously.

Here, I emphasize using the soundscape as a means to go beyond the individual experiences, the experiences one may typically have of the senses. Perceiving all the senses together is not a grand experience to reach, but it is the most basic aspect to live with, as wholeness is rooted in reality and the truth of life.

When you listen to a song or music at maximum volume with headphones or earphones on, there is nothing else one can hear except the sound of what is being played. When one looks around at such a time, everything is just happening soundlessly. But there is a movement that the eyes can see.

When the volume is turned down, the music still plays and the sound of the outside world comes into perception.

The world doesn't stop just because you stopped listening to it.

In the same way, the sound doesn't stop just because the listener isn't tuned to listen to it.
In the same way, the silence doesn't go away just because one is not rooted in it.

Sound and silence go hand in hand. They are not separate happenings, too. The paradox of existence is that everything goes with the other, and words are the only way to make another person understand the depths of life. For you to live life deeply by yourself, words are of zero significance or use.

To understand the mind, there needs to be a reflection that isn't of the mind. To see the reality of the mind, there needs to be a pure observation that is absolutely devoid of the contents of the mind. Otherwise, it is still an activity of the mind trying to understand itself, which nullifies the whole point of seeing its reality.

There is a widespread misconception that sound emerges out of silence. For sound to emerge out of silence, there needs to be sound and silence as separate entities, which is not the case. Yes, we experience silence as stillness. Yes, we experience sound as the opposite of silence. But both are not separate. The shift is so subtle that the unconscious mind will always miss it. It wants us to miss it so that we never see anything out of the activities of the mind. The silence of reality, or I will go further and say it, *the silence of the silence and the sound that emerges out are all one happening.* There is no silence without the sound, and there is no sound without the silence.
How can it be?

The mind that we experience is like a vacuum capsule in itself that allows us to experience the sound of thoughts and of the world. There are immeasurable vacuum capsules, just like you, in the form of human beings or other creations that have their own experiences of reality in the vacuum that they are born and live in. This is not something that needs proving and is as clear as daylight if a person looks at his own existence. It is the truth that you haven't yet seen.

I use the word **Nilness** to describe that which is *still* but is not only the source of everything in existence but also the ingredient of all creation. It is what gives birth to all the physical world and is also a part of it at the deepest level. **Nilness** is devoid of movement but is a part of all the movements in existence, including "The Mind of Humanity." It is part of you, too, and exists without any name.

Using the soundscape of the outer and inner world to be here in this unending moment is the simplest way to become aware of yourself and the oneness of existence. Sound is present from moment to moment, either from you or other sources in the environment. The sound of the cars, the far-off sound of the airplane going above, the sound of the keyboard when the fingers hit it as you type, the sound of the AC or the fan, the sound of a knock on the door, the sound of your breath which is subtle but still can be felt, the sound of the dog barking, the sound of fellow humans voice, the sound of all the noise around you, and at the deepest—the sound of your own thoughts.

All of this is happening at the same instant.

Whether we realize it or not in our lifetime, time only exists psychologically. Only the mind requires memory as information on which it bases the interpretations and derives meanings out of, thus creating an illusion of the past being here and of a future that doesn't exist.

Yes, we need a plan to go about life.
Yes, we need memory to remember things and people in our everyday lives.
Yes, we require experiences to differentiate what is just and what is not.
Yes, we need the contents of the mind with all its information to grow.

Most importantly, what is also necessary is the choice of keeping the mind aside when it's not needed in order to *just be* in this unbroken moment. That choice is elusive to most humans because they are too involved in enjoying the contents of the mind. That choice can only come about in one's life when one sees the limitation of the mind, its beauty, and its right place.

Too much of anything is bad to live a balanced life. However, soundscapes can be made home to come back to when one is done utilizing the contents of the mind. Soundscapes 'beauty is that they will always be there, whether you like them or not. The sound around you and within you will never disappear while you are still alive.

We do not like the noise of the traffic or noise itself because it mirrors the noise in the mind. Once there is a unity of the mind with the oneness of existence, the noise is never a problem, be it of the mind or outside.

Use sound to be in the present, unending moment, and there will come a time when the soundscape becomes your means of awakening beyond the senses—to see the oneness of existence and timelessness.

Soundscape might trigger a sudden awakening or enlightenment, where one realizes the interconnectedness of all things.

Use the sound of the external world to go deep.

Be in the most noisiest place and *observe* how they are all happening at once! They are all not separate happenings. They all take place at once.

The noise, the thoughts, the words are just a sound.

~

CHAPTER VIII — THE ART OF SENSITIVITY.
Lesson 64 — Being Sensitive.

There is a paradox of being sensitive. Sensitivity is a word, too. It is not the actual quality of being sensitive. My entire life, I have had to live with the blessing and the curse of being sensitive.

I have the deep quality of being sensitive to myself but it also comes with being sensitive to how other people are too. The closer a person is, the more intense my sensitivity is for them. I get to feel and recognize each and every shift in their mood and feelings, too.

I have found that this quality is of profound importance when it comes to spirituality and relationships. But as the saying goes— too much of anything is bad. This hits me every now and then. When my partner's mood changes, even in a conversation, that affects me in some way because I can feel the very moment there is a shift in the air between us. It is hard to describe in words because those moments are realizations, and there is no mind involved in it.

At that moment, when the shift happens, my heart has already started to pump faster, and I can feel it throbbing in my body. Then the mind takes over to spill out words in that moment of confusion of being overly sensitive about another person, which is, frankly speaking, not ours to begin with.

But the mind is such that it thrives on such moments of insecurity as it seeks security in the smallest of things in everyday life. I have experienced being sensitive as a curse when it comes to feeling other people's feelings because it is just too much to handle, as not many people live unconditionally.

Their pain becomes part of my experience in that subtle shift in the air and it comes in my way of being. This hindrance to my way of being happens because I personally love unconditionally, but I have always seen that others cannot do this all the time. They need to have conditions to be in a relationship and to go about things in life.

I function in a way that allows the growth of another person in any possible manner and flexible enough to be adaptive to their changes in the quest to grow. But the same cannot be said of other people as they live with conditions, and that damages the pure, unconditional love that life itself has for everything in it.

I have personally found that wherever there is love with conditions, there is bound to be conflicts. Conflicts between the couple and within themselves. Take any of the dialogues in the conflicts that you do have, and they resonate with hardcore beliefs, misplaced values, misunderstandings, and a sense of sabotaging that goes deep into the level of the contents of the mind.

I have read and followed spirituality deeply from 2018–2024, which began with a failure in love that I had hoped would last for life. These seven years of search with all its pain and investing myself into deeply knowing what this life is all about provided me with that solid foundation. The solid grounding allowed me to see the reality of all the contents of my mind, to see the reality of the mind, and to see the oneness of reality itself, where I realized *the mind has never been the problem.*

Where do we even hear this in our spiritual journey? The mind is seen as a problem and we go on trying to avoid it. How can you avoid something that comes with being a human? The mind itself is a problem-solving machine, and when there enters this misunderstanding that the mind is the problem, then the mind will and has to go about solving the problem of the mind being the problem. This is the root of opposing voices in the mind that are trying to solve the problem of "I am the problem." The inner conflicts and suffering are a result of seeing the mind as the problem.

I deeply realized that it was my attachment to the contents of the mind that was causing me to suffer. I could not detach myself from anything, no matter how hard I tried. One cannot be free of the contents of the mind, but we can be free of the importance we give to them. All the contents of the mind are still there, but they are not a problem anymore, as everything in existence is without time. I deeply realized that thought itself is not an independent happening but is a simultaneous occurrence along with what is on the outside too.

This breakage of boundaries between what I thought I was and what the external world was for the first 12,370 days of my life has allowed me to live in the truth, the reality. But the issue of being a human still exists as being physically alive requires one to adhere to its rules and a human body and the mind comes with it too.

The anxiety comes now and then. The human emotions exist and occur even more naturally now. The intensity of being sensitive has elevated even more so.

But with the power of sensitivity comes the responsibility of being stable. The responsibility to understand another person deeply for how they are and how they function on a moment-to-moment basis. The responsibility of taking care of my own emotions and managing it better. There also comes a choice of living life with the least amount of friction. How many actually work towards this?

Without the quality of being sensitive:

+ I am sure I would not have invested myself in spirituality.

+ I would have continued working at 9 AM to 9 PM jobs or 9

AM to 12 AM sometimes or 9 AM to the next morning 9 AM a few times—yes, I worked whenever I wasn't eating or sleeping —offering all of my time for the growth of the companies I worked for where the illusion of self-growth is at its most seductive best.

+ I would never have quit my dream job in New York, where I prioritized my peace and well-being over the abundance of money that was offered.

+ I would not have been able to reflect back on my childhood to see the traumas I went through.

+ I would not have gotten out of and over the narcissistic abuses from family members to relationships.

+ The unconditional love that I offer to my partner and the world would never have existed.

Would I ever trade back my sensitivity for anything else? Absolutely not. Sensitivity comes with its own set of pros and cons. The cons were not cons indeed when I looked at it closely, and writing is something that allowed me to let the light of the pros lit the darkness of the cons in the very process of expressing myself.

When I started writing this topic, my heart was pounding fast, and I was anxious because of the conversation I had with my partner where one of my decisions about my work was not reciprocated positively. After I poured my heart out with the words here, there is normalcy, nothing is wrong, and everything has its place.

The activities of the mind are not going to go away just because there is a realization of the oneness of existence. *Enlightenment does not take away the mind—it gives a human being an additional choice to see reality as it is without always living separately in the contents of the mind.* That switch is what makes being sensitive even more beautiful, for it allows us to experience and perceive everything as ourselves.

Sadly, there is not much sensitivity left in the world. People are rough and think it's normal. Those who are sensitive to experience or in how they live are forced to become just like the others.

To be continuously aware without any effort of what our own body is signaling is a must to keep it in good health. This can only happen by being sensitive to oneself and surroundings. Being sensitive is generally considered to be a weakness and a feminine character. This is far away from the truth. It is only by being sensitive that a human can live life with depth and perceive what being human is truly about.

Those who see sensitivity and slowness as a sign of weakness think that way since it triggers them. It triggers them when they see someone who is sensitive and slow. Looking at such a person doing the activities rather slowly than how they expect it to be done quickly to get done with it, triggers the person as they cannot stay with slowness and keep escaping from it.

How one functions within oneself is *no different* from how we end up looking at the world, how we treat people, what we talk about, what and who we get attracted to, how we behave in those small moments when people are around, and how we treat ourselves.

That person who can't take slowness from other people when there is no need to do that activity quickly is trying to replicate the very nature of the way the mind works. As they have been compulsively thinking for decades, such a programmed mind does not want to be *challenged* by a different pace of activity than how it itself functions.

The mind looks for reaffirmations to ground its already established patterns even deeper. Here is where the safety of the mind lies. Anything that threatens it, even as small a thing as slowness from somebody outside, triggers the heck out of it as it cannot withstand something that would collapse its entire structure on which it is based on. This is why not many can sit down just by themselves without doing anything.

Such a mind does not *yet* know what it is to be flexible, how beautiful it is to grow outside of our beliefs, and certainly cannot know love, as everything it does arises out of fear in thousands of different ways on an everyday basis. This feels like something that cannot be altered because that person does not *yet* know any other way to be or hasn't had a healthy exposure to the normal way of existing. I use the word *yet* for the mind not yet knowing a different way to approach life on top of which it can base itself healthily rather than being compulsive. The capability to be sensitive is in all of us if only we melt a little and become vulnerable—to all that we have gone through, to all the pains, to all the miseries, to all the regrets, to all the unfixable things of the past, and most importantly to all the qualities we do have without shunning or strengthening them—as being sensitive itself brings in a natural order of its own qualities that are enough to live deliberately.

~

Lesson 65 — How You Are Is How You Do Everything.

As much as you don't want to see it, how you go about doing things externally is *exactly* how you are on the inside. By inside, I mean the very qualities of you.

It is a mirror that cannot be seen, but it does exist formlessly in the activities that you do. All that is done looks completely different on the surface level when you see it with these mortal eyes, but when looked at deeply, you are doing each and everything as a by-product of how you truly are.

Though this might seem very complex at first, there are things that you do in a certain way and things that you like doing naturally. You like doing them without any effort because you really like doing that thing. Nobody has to tell you to do it, but as default, you keep going back to this one thing. On your own.

If you like slowness, you will enjoy watching the clouds, the stars, the sky, nature, animals, and everything that is slow by design. Even the dust settles down slowly but since you have the sensitivity and awareness, the slow falling down of a single dust can be observed and be conscious about. If you can enjoy the settling down of a speck of dust, that means in your very innate human nature, there is a pull towards all that is slow in nature. This pull is the flow of life trying to guide you to move towards the things that will make you perceive beyond the senses—the deepest realizations you can have. It takes time from the human growth point of view, but as you grow deeper and deeper to observe life consciously, there comes a deep awe of what life is all about, of what everything around you is about, and of what you are. You need to actually see all this to get an essence of this way of living deeply.

You might like to clean on the outside and keep things tidy. This is how you are innately, too, as the mind creates order out of all the chaos and randomness, just like you clean up your room and desk before sitting down to do your work.

You may feel a pull towards living a simple life. This is because you are simple in your heart, in your wantings and needs. Such a person does not need a lot of things to live on a daily basis. It has everything to do with how you are within yourself, the experiences that you have gone through and made yourself go through in order to want a simple life.

You may wish to have all the material wealth of the world and keep working day in and day out. This is because there is a deep unfulfillment of needs that were not or are not being met. It is not a bad thing to desire a materialistic life, but *the roots are not in what you are desiring but in what you are deeply* that shows up in the form of desires.

You want to be with a loving partner because there is a need for love that you so badly want to be fulfilled since you haven't been able to do it yourself.

To feel complete is a filling of the void about something by somebody or something else. Though it does not solve the problem of unfulfillment at the root level, the filling of the void by something or somebody does the patch-up work temporarily till life challenges you and leaves you with no option but to work on yourself and look at why the void exists in the first place.

Life challenges you because you haven't addressed the existence of the emptiness. This emptiness at the deepest level is **Nilness** that has been flowing even before you were born and even after you die. It does not know death.

When you come to a point of realization and touch this true reality of the mirror that exists in how you are and what you do, the mind has no option but to come to terms with the deep acceptance and tag along without posing itself as a problem but as a friend who helps you out whenever you require his aid. The mind will be there to assist you when you consciously choose to use it.

The reality is how you are and all that you come with. When you sync completely with how you are, it is a natural flow of life to take you to where you naturally belong as a piece of life. This ends up directing you to shift doing what you do for work to something that is in line with what comes naturally to you without any friction from the mind.

This is when you live a frictionless life *doing* what you are, and the separation falls away.

~

Lesson 66 — Sound of Silence.

When one observes or looks or sees, which is very different from focusing and being intense about something, there is a sound that cannot be heard in that silence. That is the sound of silence that existence is. It is a happening.

When something is happening, nothing can be done in that moment and can only be talked about later on as to what happened. The key to unlocking the oneness with the rest of existence lies in becoming one with the happenings.

When one becomes simple enough to look at the slowly passing clouds and stay with that observation without wording anything in the mind, that is when reality is actually seen.

+ When one can simply look at the squirrels hopping over the tree without *thinking*, there's the reality.

+ When one can simply see the swaying leaves of a tree and stay in that moment without interpreting anything, there's the reality.

+ When one is just *aware* of a passing butterfly or an insect or an ant or a bird, without talking about it in the mind or with anybody else, there's the reality.

There is a greater depth in observing on our own without another by our side. It can also be done with anybody around, but the depth of observation will depend on how conscious you are.

The reality is even there when there is speech, but if and only if the person is conscious of what they are saying.

Reality can be observed when a person sees the thoughts for what it is and doesn't go on to give them much importance as it corrupts the view.

A person under intense emotions can also look without thinking, but in that state, there is a filter of the emotion that they are in, which obstructs the view of reality. The reality has no human emotions and doesn't care for what it is being thought about.

+ Reality just exists.

+ The clouds just pass by.

+ The birds fly.

+ The ants march on.

+ Humans keep building and destroying.

+ Earth stays in motion, and the sun keeps lighting it up day in and day out.

+ The existence keeps existing.

+ All you can really do is attune yourself to the sound of silence, which is a gateway to all realizations.

~

Lesson 67 — Observation.

One can perceive **Nilness** through a number of simple but effective ways.

Rain:

+ Looking at the droplets of water falling down.

+ Completely immerse yourself without a care about the world around you by paying attention to the observable shower and the unobservable place that it is pouring from the sky.

+ Coming to the realization of how glorious the whole system of our planet is to keep providing its occupants with the environment to grow and flourish.

Clouds:

+ Look up to the clouds that we have free access to. We don't need to pay to look at them as one would to look at a movie created by us humans. Clouds are the most serene and the most beautiful layers of our human existence. It is right there to be seen, and most of us miss that too.

+ Clouds move slowly. A person wouldn't enjoy watching the clouds if the mind is rampaging at full speed. How the mind is and what we want to look at on the outside mirrors in ways one has no idea about. If one does not have the quality of slowness and sensitivity, observing the clouds would be equivalent to a waste of time as they get nothing out of it. *When there is nothing to gain, there is everything to gain out of it.*

+ Only the mind that knows stillness and slowness can appreciate the slow passing by of the clouds that are never in a hurry. The whole existence is never in a hurry—everything happens slowly. Your body, too, didn't just come out into the world with how you are now. It took time to grow, little by little. Observe those white clouds that are enormous and gigantic in size and wonder without the filters of the mind.

Breath:

+ The first breath we take is when we come into this world. The last breath is our exit. Realize that there are only so many breaths in between, and take them slowly and consciously. Be aware of each and every breath. Breathing is a paradox, too. You do it, and you can't stop not doing it.

+ We can breathe because there is air around that the body takes in to keep itself alive and continue its activities right down to the cells. This taking in and breathing out air is itself proof that we are not independent of what is around us. The body is dependent on the environment to remain alive, to sustain itself, and to keep all of its mechanisms going. We cannot exist individually without the air that the plants provide us. Mother Earth took billions of years to get the precise amount of oxygen —still a word named by us humans—that you are breathing right now. This is no small feat.

+ You are interconnected with all that is on Earth, which is why there are pandemics that affect the entire human population when something goes haywire in the very air that our mortal bodies live in. Add all the other living organisms on the planet and we can get an idea of how complex a system it is we call home. Observe. Be grateful for each and every breath and appreciate all that has happened and that is happening to let you continue breathing without having to ask for air.

Plants and trees:

+ The green color is so enriching to our eyes that our body craves for it intrinsically because it is made out of Earth. That which we come from, we have to go back to it. We *can* breathe as there are plants and trees in the world. They are the main source apart from the sun that made it possible for life to begin in the first place.

+ Though we as humanity have disrespected Mother Earth in the most terrible ways, you, as a single sensible human being, can pay respect to it by looking at the tree in front of your house without the activity of the mind. Can you do this much? When you look at it, do not talk about it or think about the tree, or the leaves, or the breeze that moves it. Just look at the tree without any words or thoughts. That is you, paying respect to the life that it has offered to you to be alive and goes on giving it.

+ Trees are the heart of our little existence here on Earth. They are not just the food that we eat. They are the reason that you are alive right now, this very second. Trees cannot walk. They gently swing with the breeze and come back to their original position. There is a great deal of presence in them if one observes deeply. Those leaves and the branches moving, deeply mirror and occur in unison with your very thoughts, too, or the silence when the mind isn't operating.

Heartbeat:

+ The sound of our heart. Oh, what a means to be in touch with reality. This is your own heart beating, and you listening to the sound of it. Are you listening to it without having to place your hands to feel it?

+ One of the beautiful ways to see your own reality and come out of the contents of the mind is by being in touch with the body. I refer to coming out of the compulsive mind here in those who are yet to see the mind for what it is. One can hear the sound of the heart thumping with roughly similar intensity as the thoughts if one observes its beating. Just being aware that there is a heart beating inside you increases the sound of it in your awareness. The sound of the heart beating has always been there, but it is only you who has been unaware of it. Listen to your own heart beating.

+ The sound of the heartbeat. The sound of a thought emerging. The sound of the rain pouring down. The sound and the silence of the breath, the clouds, the breath—are all happening simultaneously.

All of it has different intensities, but deeply observing to hear and see that there is no difference in the happenings as all of them are occurring at the same instant makes one aware of the fact of reality that there is no other moment that has ever occurred or there is no next moment that is going to occur. This unending moment is the reality, one that is without time, and yet we see things growing physically. This is the paradox of that which exists and that which allows it to.

Words:

When we speak, that is a sound coming out in the form of words. Words are sound, too. This is rarely observed.

Thoughts:

Thought is a sound. There is nothing more to it. We generate each and every thought. You are just not aware that you are the one doing it. It doesn't happen on its own. Observe deeply, and you will clearly see that you are the one giving birth to each and every thought.

Observing the oneness of existence:

There is no journey in observing the truth and the oneness of existence. All one can do to be one with it is observe. The pain of living separate from the oneness of existence is only realized when the oneness is observed.

When such fundamental aspects of reality are not in our perception, it is obvious to live and get lost in the psychological world that the mind creates.

People function with conditionings in the background, which is to say, living on top of already existing beliefs, which are not the reality but a pattern of the mind.

Allow yourself to grow as a person in a way that inculcates experiencing day-to-day life with *all* the senses and the mind coming together to live in reality as it is. To live in the truth moment-to-moment.

The real question is whether one continues living in the dream or wakes up. There is tremendous comfort in living in the illusions of the mind, and it requires deep observation to wake up and see reality.

~

Lesson 68 — The Art of Looking.

Seeing or looking is not *thinking.*

When you want to only see, you must be *able* to just see, be it something within yourself or externally. This is when there are no images created from the bundle of memories. It is only in this way that a human being can look at their own reality as they end up staring at reality directly. It becomes quite obvious.

The problem with an unconscious person is that he is not *aware* that he himself is responsible for the thoughts that seem to go on on their own.

He is not aware that *he* is *thinking!*

It is *he* who gives birth to every single thought that has ever occurred in the mind.

It is *he* who goes on thinking endlessly, which then creates anxiety and turmoil within the system.

The moment he realizes and becomes aware of a simple fact that he gives birth to his very own thoughts and makes it a habit to be aware of the thoughts that arise, without doing anything about it, the thoughts can be seen for what they are.

In the unconscious mind, the thoughts come about from existing memories, which is the past, and the person is unaware.

In a conscious person, he is aware, and it is *he* who generates the thoughts that he wants to think at any given moment. Any wavering thoughts that pass by are just looked at without giving any significance to it. To such a person, he becomes aware of the thinking that happens unconsciously. That's it.

Just becoming aware of such thoughts ends the stream of unconscious thinking. But the same is not the case in a person who is not conscious, where the stream of thoughts goes on without any end in sight, which creates havoc, first to the person within himself and then onto the world, even if it is just the small world of that individual.

The world at large that exists today is the consequence of the united play of different states of the mind. This is the simple truth. The mind that agreed came together, and those that didn't turned to other places where it was more in tune with, irrespective of whether it did it for security, safety, happiness, or any other factors. Such an amalgam of the mind that concurred is what created separateness from those that didn't concur. *We call them countries.*

What we see in the world today is how human beings have been.

How we are as a person is what defines an individual's life, and whether that is a life of conscious way of living or not makes the utmost difference in its quality. Those who end up living life deeply have full-blown experiences and perceptions of what humanity and being human is all about. They see its limitations and its enormous connection with everything that exists. It is only then that they start creating a life that is as frictionless as possible with the truth of life in sight, with their own natural innate qualities by the side, and with this present unending moment of reality as the foundation of living.

Each and every human experience serves as a gateway to awareness when there is a conscious looking. When it is there, the human experience of even the smallest of things becomes consciousness itself and there is no separating the two as they are no different at all when looked at consciously. But the unconscious mind will always make it two and get lost in its world of words and experiences.

While you read this, there is an inescapable interpretation of what the conscious and the unconscious mind could be, which sounds like two since different words are being used. But they are not two in terms of existence. There is a difference only in the depth of the mind.

The unconscious refers to the contents that run in the background that one is not aware of.

The conscious refers to the contents that one is aware of.
There is only a difference in whether you are perceiving it or not perceiving the reality.
Awareness—If you look at the reality of the mind, you live in reality and are conscious.
Unawareness—If you do not look at the reality of the mind, then you are in the contents of the unconscious mind that you have allowed and are allowing to dictate all of your life.

When looking at a well, the end of which cannot be seen when looking from the top of the well, we do not call it the deep well and the top well. It's just a well with depth—some we can see and the deepest we cannot. The mind is also one component, and it is a word that we humans worded out for our understanding. There is no need to get attached to the words and further divide them while we are understanding the different aspects of the mind.

A gentle reminder that the *word* mind is *not* the mind. The mind cannot be the word we have used for the purpose of communicating about it. The mind is entirely different and only comes into perception when looked at with awareness.

This is the English language that I use to write to convey information in order to bring awareness into day-to-day and moment-to-moment life as you read these words. The words consciousness, awareness, looking, and observing are all used to mean the same thing, but as they are different words, their meanings are interpreted differently in different contexts. The words *act* as the medium to first understand what is being talked about and then bring it into one's life. That is all the role of words is.

Coming back to looking consciously, it doesn't happen when there is haste, and there is haste because you don't allow slowness in anything, which in turn completely disrupts the gateway of awareness to look consciously.

It's a cycle, and if one does not come out of it, there will be no depth in the experiences as the cycle keeps repeating. The cycle continues as there is haste.

Looking consciously ≠ Haste.

Looking consciously = Slowness.

Looking consciously = Stillness.

Look up, and you will notice that the clouds don't rush. They flow. How can you be different from it? What you see is nature, and the natural design of nature is no different from how you are designed. There is suffering when there is no alignment of the mind with the natural design and functioning of a human being.

If we look at it deeply, the form of nature is no different from ours, which is why we keep going back to it, feeling good and connected.

But how often do we reflect as to what is that which is connecting?
What is indeed connecting is the flow of life which is not different, be it what you see in the capacities as a human or of the human itself.

The flow of life is always at ease. It can never be disrupted.

At times, when you slow down and sit by yourself, your breath is slow and at a natural pace with the air outside of your body. This is there by default, and you need not put effort into it. The mind has slowed down in that moment from all its processing and compulsive thinking. Sitting on a chair, you feel connected with something beyond your physicalness. The same happens when you are in nature. That connection is ever-flowing, and it is only the over-involvement and attachment with the contents of the mind that destroys the connection with the flow and brings out haste in our day-to-day lives.

~

CHAPTER IX — THE ART OF BEING HERE.
Lesson 69 — Mind with Reality.

Once you come to a point where you are aware you are doing it, where you are aware that you are the one who is thinking, and it is not the brain or the mind, the separation becomes one.

This is not a one-time event where you see it, and it will stay permanently. The battle of the mind—regaining control over the present unending moment using any of the stored information—with the awareness of being right here in this moment is a constant marathon for those who are unaware and feel like a war that lasts a lifetime. But this is not the kind of war where there is revenge, competition, dominance, differences, or strong identities.

This is a dance between the creator and the creation for those who see it.

There also comes a point where the war ends, and you know entirely that there is no separation. But the nature of the mind is such that even those who have seen reality are affected by its innate design. The mind separates and splits everything into categories for it to have safety and existence *in time*, that is, in the thoughts and memories related to past experiences.

The Art of Nilness takes root when there is a balance and harmony of the mind existing with reality and you being here, perceiving the wonders and beauty of life.

~

Lesson 70 — The Art of Being Here.

Use the present unending moment as a platform for discovering the subtlety of the mind.

Consciously questioning the happenings of the mind is a gentle way of using the mind itself to let it reveal its complexity.

Being open to all possibilities psychologically is an important aspect because the mind that has been unconscious for decades just doesn't let go of the survival mechanisms that it has built up over time. But when one is open to seeing whatever the mind is doing, *that* is the first ray of the light that has the power to turn the mind from being unaware to aware and marks the start of a juggernaut.

The mind will keep referring back to all the memories of the past, be it anything. It will fore up the hurt, the pain, the difficult experiences, the happy moments, or any random thought that has its link with what has already occurred in the past to bring in a new emotional freshness & reaffirmation to what is being experienced *now*. Do you see how the mind, with all its contents, *will do anything and everything* to not let you just *be* in this moment, which is all there is in reality?

The nature of the mind is to exist and keep humans safe and protected. To keep existing, the mind needs to keep playing its recorder, just as you do physically by eating the food for the body to exist. If you had no record playing in the mind, what else would the mind be doing in all that freed-up space?

Nothing. It *can* exist without playing its recorder. The fact is that the mind *can* exist without playing its contents and that *you* can use its contents as and when necessary. You already have seen this, where in moments of awe, there are no words in the mind— that is, perceiving reality without the mind obstructing it with its contents.

The body needs food to survive, and it leaves out unwanted materials and only uses what the body requires or is capable of retaining. But the mind has *no such* filters for the incoming information. It retains everything. This is its nature, and right from childhood it has grown in proportion and complexities by connecting what it has received to what has worked for it. This has a profound effect on the way a person is. The connections and meanings it adds to all of its information, be it of the past or what it is receiving now, are simply staggering if one becomes aware of it. We do need the function of the mind to survive on a day-to-day basis, but what needs to be undone are the patterns out of those meanings that are not necessary.

Information → Meaning → Pattern

Examples of patterns that are self-defeating:

Example:

A kid wants a toy, and he asks for it.
The parents do not buy.
The kid cries.
The parents buy the toy for the kid.

Information: I want the toy.
Meaning: I get the toy if I cry for it.
Pattern: I will repeat it to get my next toy. [This pattern continues into adulthood for various things.]

Example:

A college student skips classes and goes to explore the cyber world.
She lies to her parents that she has been going to college.
Her parents do not go to validate her statements. She continues going to the cybercafe.

Information: I want to go to a cybercafe.
Meaning: I can go to cybercafe instead of college.
Pattern: I will continue lying to my parents as they do not go to find out where I am.

Example:

Ashley has been cheated on in her past relationships.
She stays committed to the person, but she often finds herself with partners who are likely to cheat on her.
She remains in the relationship even after being cheated on and abused.
The way she copes with it is by trying to get herself to be okay with being cheated on and that she loves her partner more than just his body.

Information: I am cheated on and abused by my partner.
Meaning: It is okay to be cheated on.
Pattern: I love him more than his body.

The more number of times the pattern has been re-affirmed, the deeper it gets ingrained. The deeper it is engrained, the harder it is to see it. The harder it is to see it, the higher the degree of unawareness. But the power of awareness is such that it doesn't matter how deep the meaning has been established—awareness can flush it out in an instant. The point is not that a person will be left with meaninglessness. The meanings that are of the mind are made up as a coping mechanism to the external world and internal sufferings. It just doesn't have any relation to reality, which is why it needs constant validation to keep it afloat. Reality doesn't give a damn about re-affirmation. It doesn't need any of it. It is just there. It is the unconscious mind that keeps trying to exist with its contents that are actually not required most of the time.

Examples of patterns that serve its purpose:

+ There are patterns that do help in daily living.

Example:

There is a huge pothole in the middle of the road right after Ethan leaves his new home.
The first time, he ended up going right over it, which damaged the wheels and the suspension of the vehicle but more

importantly, caused injury to Ethan.

The next time he takes that road, he remembers there is a pothole and drives around it to avoid what happened the last time.

Information: There is a pothole on the road.
Meaning: I need to avoid hitting the pothole to save myself from getting injured and the vehicle from the damages.
Pattern: I will drive around the pothole.

+ There are new meanings to old patterns that help us in getting over old harmful patterns.

Example:

Ben has been drinking alcohol for the last 10 years.

Information: I like drinking alcohol.
Meaning: I like to party, enjoy myself, and get high.
Pattern: I want to go to the pub and drink more alcohol than any of my friends.

On one such night, he was rushed to the emergency room after an intense pain in his upper right abdomen. The doctors diagnosed him with Alcohol-Related Liver Disease. After a week-long treatment at the hospital, Ben came back home and decided to stop drinking and chose to live a healthier lifestyle.

Information: I am addicted to alcohol.
New meaning: If I continue drinking alcohol, I might damage my body permanently.
New pattern: I will stop drinking alcohol and live healthily.

+ There is also an innate sense of discovering patterns in order to stop their influence on our lives.

Example:

Continuing the story of Ashley, one day, it hits her that she is free to leave the relationship if she is not respected. That she is better off without a partner who doesn't see her worth and the value she brings to the relationship. She ends the relationship as she wishes to be with a person with whom she can have a deep connection.

Information: I am disrespected in the relationship.
New meaning: I can walk out freely since my partner doesn't value me and my need for a monogamous relationship.
New pattern: I will end the relationship to be with someone whom I can deeply connect with.

Information is memory, and memory is information. Information that comes in is stored as memory to reflect on later, consciously or unconsciously. How the memory is reflected back on has a great effect on how a person is in this present unending moment. There is a huge repository of memories which contain a lot of information primarily stored as per the individual's identification with the memories.

Just as the building block of a human body is a cell, the building block of the past is information. Yes, there are many words used to precisely describe the memories, emotions, experiences, etc., but at the depth of it all, there is information that the mind has wrapped up into meanings which become a pattern as time passes by.

Being in this present unending moment is nothing but allowing information to pass right by us wherein we are not influenced by it, but we *do* use the information and act upon it. Whatever the information, be it from another person, a resource, nature, or the mind, we simply observe, look at it, and act on it consciously.

Information → No meaning → No patterns

Example:

Jane is frustrated that she gets disturbed every morning. She tells her husband Jacob angrily, "I do not function normally when my sleep is disturbed at 5 AM when you open the room door. I need my 8 hours of sleep. For god sake, do not lock the door back."

Now, Jacob could have yelled back at her for jumping on him and for not mentioning it before they slept. But he is aware that his wife requires sleep and acknowledges the sound that wakes her up in the morning. Jacob tells her, "I am sorry. I will keep the door open and make as little sound as possible."

Information: Jane's 8-hour sleep schedule is disturbed when I wake up at 5 AM by locking back the room door, which makes a loud noise.
Solution: I will not lock the room's door next time.

Information → No meaning → No pattern → Solution.

What Jacob did in that heated moment was *use* the *information* that was coming his way, but he *did not assign* any meaning to what his wife was saying which cuts off any pattern that could have existed. The most important part of how Jacob handled the situation was by seeing the information as information and nothing else attached to it, which brings in the mindset of finding a solution instantly.

Information → Solution.

When it comes to just you, there is a lot of information lingering around in the mind. They keep popping to the surface in our day-to-day lives.

When it pops up, *look* at it.

What is the thought that has suddenly appeared out of nowhere and seems to be something that you have not played any role in its popping up?

Let it play out.

Observe what the thought is about.

Largely, the thoughts that come up have a mechanism running in the background to *repeat* what the mind already knows. Amongst the rubble of information, the mechanisms that are firmly established and which the mind has learned to have security with play out *automatically* as if it is the only way. But it is not the only way. The default mechanisms or patterns have been *set* as default by the mind itself as it worked out in the past to cope with those particular circumstances. By re-iterating these *set* patterns, the mind reaffirms that this is the way to survive.

Thoughts are not good or bad by themselves. It is the meaning that we assign to those thoughts that derive a paradoxical sense of righteousness and wrongdoings. Thoughts are there to aid humans in learning, problem-solving, expressing, identifying, reasoning, and planning, which let us live, connect with others, and prosper. Thoughts also help us in navigating decisions, setting goals, achieving them, and understanding the way we are. What I am currently doing is expressing my thoughts consciously to share with whoever ends up reading this.

We can go on reasoning about the contents of the mind, but it is still the mind describing itself, which is paradoxical, as is everything else if looked at deeply. There are times when using the mind is a necessity, and then there are times when its usefulness has no place. This becomes crystal clear when one learns to implement **The Art of Nilness** in day-to-day life and moment-to-moment presence.

~

Lesson 71 — Awareness.

Get done with the process of knowing in order to get something back. It may help in achievements, fame, a great boost to the egoistic mind, and survival. But knowledge does not and can never will—let a human see that which is unattainable.

Get done with enlightenment.

Put a full stop to enlightenment or anything else that is on your radar to reach. Only then do the necessary work.

Enlightenment cannot be attained. It can only be arrived at without a start or an end.

Fulfillment isn't only in the amount of money we have beyond survival but in the essence of being completely in sync with ourselves, which, in turn, is in sync with reality. Because what cannot be explained in words, but nevertheless, the words do try, is that the observable and the hidden reality exist in plain sight. Every. Single. Moment. Not only in what the human eyes can see but in every nook and corner of reality. You can call it the universe or god or yourself. It doesn't freaking care. To it, there is no time.

The unattainable is timeless.

The mind can *only* exist with time as its foundation—in the past memories and projecting the future. This is why so much importance is given to the present unending moment. If one can be here, right here, and keep being here, the mind or thinking stops to exist in that moment when the person is present, and hence, there is no essence of time.

But the majority of humans exist in a psychological time that makes it impossible to observe what is hidden right in front of them—not even at the other end of the world, where they have no access to, but something that lives and throbs right in front and with them from the moment they were born to start existing. The reality becomes more and more oblivious as the mind starts to be at the fore and goes from strength to strength with the information it has been fed. What it ends up making meaning out of all the information is stored deeply for survival. This resistance, or rather a lack of adaptability of a dogmatic mind *to* change in spite of the crystal clear healthier alternatives, is *exactly* what puts a person against the tide in which life flows. This is why all of the human sufferings exist.

A whole lot of humanity lives with suffering throughout their life span.
How can such an environment teach a growing child to see the truth?
How can the people around a newborn who have no clue what the mind is and what it does to them, how can these people bring up a child consciously?
How can a child not suffer when everyone around is suffering?
How can there be peace in the world when this cycle of unaware parents raising a new generation of unaware kids continues?
The cycle can stop only when enough people become conscious and choose to see reality to break out of the compulsiveness of the mind.

The definition of compulsiveness, as per the Cambridge Dictionary:
"behavior in which someone does something too much and is unable to stop doing it."

The reality of how much the mind shapes a person is much much deeper as it is wired to an entire knowledge base, and to keep that knowledge aside—even for a while—is what troubles everybody.

When you drink water from a bottle, you are *able* to keep the bottle back down after drinking the water. Wouldn't it be a problem if, after using it for the first time, the bottle stuck to the mouth and didn't come out? Because you have the ability to *use* the water bottle whenever you want to, you *can* pick it up and keep it down. The same must have been the case with using the mind, but it isn't so.

The mind picks up information or knowledge from the outside right from childhood constantly. Since there is nobody to even say that it is alright to keep the information aside for a while, the memories, the beliefs, and all that come up from an individual's past get so firmly *stuck* to the person that they have no idea they *can* live without it, where there is no difference between their sense of self and their *thinking*, the thinking that is constantly occurring from all the knowledge as its base. This is a recipe for disaster sooner or later. The person may think they are very successful and invincible, but even to such people life has its ways of letting them know about its truth.

Life or god or truth or reality, word it whatever, is, in short—a play of hide and seek.

The truth has hidden itself everywhere and expects to be found.

It will be revealed to those who first realize that there is a game that is being played, who then go forth to find the truth only to come to an awareness that—*You are it, and it is you.* There is no freaking difference, distance, division whatsoever.

Let that sink in. Read it a hundred times if you must.

I repeat. Let. That. Sink. In.

You are it, and it is you.

Life is a duality. Both spectrums exist. But the imbalance that exists in the human world is quite enormous for anybody to see. This is why it is more urgent to look into ourselves first, throw out the patterns that the mind has been clinging to for decades on end, and finally—change.

Mind is not a man's enemy. It becomes an enemy when it starts working against us as there is a lack the awareness and touch with reality. Seeing that the mind has been compulsive is the first step towards a journey that will bring about an irrevocable change. Once we see a glimpse of what reality is, the truth of it starts to enter the core of our being. If you are serious about finding out, if there is willingness and surrender at the same time, you will put in effort and be effortless at the same time.

A glimpse of reality is all it takes to put a person on a journey without any need for a destination. Words fall short epically to describe what reality is.

The actual reality, or if you want to call it life, *cannot* be worded out. Period.

As the body goes through recovery when it is sick, the diseased-unconscious-conditioned mind, too, when reality starts to seep in, goes through rejection and attacks to protect what it has built for decades. For example, this is quite evident when a person is told something against their beliefs and they defend it. Please see that it is *not* the person defending it, but it is their inflexible mind defending itself when put in a spot of bother against its rigid mental authority. This can be seen in day-to-day conversations with a family member, a partner, a colleague, or with literally anybody who has the mind, which is everybody. Isn't it funny that when one sees reality, in order to protect the unconscious contents, the mind clings to its rigid principles and fights when there comes a point to drop them? But the light of reality is so powerful that it does not stop unless the person becomes *aware* of what the mind is doing.

The awareness of the compulsive mind puts an end to its compulsive motion, be it anything. Be it any damn thing in the realm of thinking or imagination. It may start to revolt in order to protect a belief that is strong. See your own actions, behavior, and thought process when this happens. Usually, the statement in favor of a particular belief comes ashore during the defense. When it comes ashore—*shine the light of awareness for it to end.* This is all that's needed. This is not magic, religious, or even spiritual. It is just a conscious response to something that has been happening unconsciously for way too long in your own life.

There is a reason why we tend to stay away from pitch-black

darkness, and that is because we cannot see anything. It scares us and makes us feel unsafe as to what will happen. Once the lights are switched on, there is a sigh of not being in danger anymore. Only then can a person walk freely.

The same is the case with a compulsive mind which has lived in the darkness of its contents. Once there is a light of awareness, or if you want to call it consciousness, the mind is no longer scared as it realizes there is no danger anymore and eases off the grip on its contents, be it whatever. Only then can there be a free mind that doesn't resist change.

To state it briefly:

Pitch darkness = Contents of the mind.
Cannot see visually = Cannot see mentally.
Danger of walking in darkness = Danger of clinging to the contents of the mind.
Switch on lights = Switch on awareness.
Walk freely = A free mind.

The next question someone might have is, if it is the mind doing all this then what or who is the person using the mind?
When there is a free mind, to such a person, there is no distinction between themselves or the activities of the mind or the reality itself.

Words are tricky, but to pen it down—

You are the Awareness.

It is not even a state of being but that which becomes aware of itself.

~

CHAPTER X — THE ART OF NILNESS.

We can only verbally talk about **The Art of Nilness**, but we can never do the same about **Nilness** without corrupting what it is. Everything that is obstructing **Nilness** itself needs to be seen first, then eliminated, and there it will be to be looked at with awareness. It cannot come to the fore of your life if there are barriers that haven't been eliminated in some way or the other.

+ Accepting and understanding the world as it is.

+ Understanding your place in the world.

+ Respecting the earthly body that each one of us comes with into this world.

+ Being aware of all the various ways a human system functions.

+ Being here to see the truth of relationships with oneself, other people, and the world.

+ Seeing the limitations of all the creations of the mind.

+ Developing the innate qualities through the lens of **Nilness** to live existentially with reality.

+ Building healthy connections with others.

+ Living in balance.

+ Living deliberately.

Nilness is not something one can get to. Once you see it, the subtle nature and usefulness of it as a human being, the **Nilness** can become a way of living in the unending moment in our daily, seemingly mundane life but one that is full of beauty.

Nilness is not something to be achieved, interpreted, or experienced. It can only be perceived when all the senses come together with reality.

There is no place as to where the perception takes place. It cannot be pinpointed as it doesn't exist in the realm of human reasoning and languages. When one has an understanding of something or experiences it, it is coming from a view point of a human experience. Even if it is the highest form of experience, it still is in the limited human experience.

An unconscious person reading this using the mind cannot get this limitation of being human, as it contradicts their experience of life until now. It can be startling to see what else can be there other than experiencing life. The truth is that when one is conscious, the whole viewpoint of how everything is perceived is elevated, not in terms of the level of experience as most people may think of as, but in the simplicity of living deeply with the entire existence, which is beyond the scope of the limited human mind and yet within the potential of what it is to be a human and see it all.

~

Lesson 72 — Thinking.

Thinking is energy spent towards something, just as a physical activity that requires energy.

Not a lot of people make themselves aware of such a simple fact of where their energy gets depleted throughout the day. Just because thinking is not seen by anybody else, over time, the person creates a safe haven where anything can be spoken and seen. There is nobody to witness whether the words spoken or the images imagined are acceptable in the outside world.

Such a sense of false independence lets the person build meanings, interpretations, defenses, memories, mechanisms, systems, repetitions, repressions, identities, and a sense of self that is separate from what is outside their body.

Some of these are necessary for particular scenarios, but 95% of the thinking is leaked out without any need or hold over the immense energy spent in that direction.

By learning **The Art of Nilness**, one can first come to that space where it is possible to be free of external influences and internal sufferings. A human being can remain with **Nilness** and *choose* to spend their energy that is not out of compulsiveness and patterns but that which blossoms out of deep awareness and perception.

~

Lesson 73 — Perception.

There are very few words that haven't been corrupted yet in so many different ways. When people realize there is an opportunity to make money with entertainment such as meditation, spirituality, religion, god, etc., one can clearly see there is a rush towards it and make varieties out of it.

But when it comes to—observing themselves, looking at their own lives and patterns, being free of their past, getting over their mental blocks, doing what they know in their gut they must be doing, and bettering their quality of life inwardly —things such as these and many, many more can never be corrupted by society because it is about *You!*

It is possible to make yourself and other people miserable through your actions and way of life, but the *subtleties* of what makes you a human being and **The Art of Looking** at those subtle innate nature of yourself can never ever be corrupted.

This is why it has been sought after by all humans throughout history and for the very reason that very few people get to those subtleties of human nature is what makes it *the most valuable discovery* in the entire span of a human life.

Those rare people who do end up living deeply see the true nature of everything.

They get to that point only because of the realization of how limited human experiences are and, at the same time, how immense and beautiful it is to *perceive* all the illusions and still go on playing it—being at the edge of everything an organism such as us can possibly comprehend.

~

Lesson 74 — Question Everything.

It is a beautiful day to be alive.

To be listening to the rain that has been pouring for hours on end.

It is a beautiful day to be grateful for having good enough health and mindset.

It is an even more beautiful day to be alive, to exist along with the rest of existence, and to be writing out of sheer consciousness.

Do you need more reasons to have a beautiful day?

How about taking a walk early in the morning and being in touch with the space around your body? That sounds wonderful, doesn't it? There is a part of us that wants to be more than this body, and at the same time there is a part of us that *has* to be in this body to be able to experience as a human being.

Why do we feel the presence of something greater than the body we have?

That is because what we are in this human form is not forever. It is not an eternal, immortal form. We are the result of randomness with structure. A structure that was shaped over billions of years on the very planet we come out of. We are, in a sense, "The Children of Earth," a Mother who has given birth to all the living and non-living entities that have a life of their own, and that includes a human life too, wherein each one of us has our own apparently unique life but always connected to everything else.

Without the support of the body, which arose out of iterative adaptations, we wouldn't be experiencing what we do today. We wouldn't even be able to breathe, and our hearts wouldn't be beating one beat without the explicit preciseness of Mother Nature's design that has allowed us to come to form and to the point of questioning, "Who am I?"

It cannot get more intimate than this—something that has arisen out of creation has reached a stage of questioning who created it, how it was created, and why it was created.

This ability to question and ponder is what makes us human beings so connected to our creator.

The creator who not only gave birth to our own Mother but to the Mothers of all other entities that our eyes will never get to see.

The creator who is at the core of everything and hidden from the limelight and which comes to the fore when the creation— a human being like you and me—questions what has been told to us and thereafter deeply questions everything, including this very body and the mind that we use on a moment-to-moment basis.

+ Question whether we are mere flesh or something greater than that.

+ Question why we feel the need to keep expanding ourselves in various ways.

+ Question—who is it really that is looking through these mortal eyes?

~

Lesson 75 — Live Deliberately: With Writing.

When every human experience becomes a gateway to **Nilness** and back, that is when you drop my writings completely and are ready to live deliberately with no intentions of your own.

Simplicity is the most common quality and at the core of all those who have brought about a change in our world for the betterment. Take anybody—Steve Jobs, Gandhi, Mother Teresa, Abdul Kalam, J Krishnamurthi, Bill Gates, Warren Buffett—and you will notice that on a day-to-day basis, these people, although they may come off as rich, successful, and fortunate, chose simplicity to live by. The fame may blur this out, but for those who truly see their lives, there is simplicity in everything they did for the world and in how they lived.

Writing is not as difficult as people think it is. At the same time, it is not easy either, so most people tend to move towards skills that do not involve reflecting or expressing themselves. Even though those skills may be more challenging to master than simply allowing themselves to sit, reflect, and write, most people choose not to do that which is simple.

To write is an art.
It is not just scribbling all the thoughts that come up.
Writing can become a healing process, too. As you write, your own reality begins to reveal.
Writing with awareness by your side is the deepest form of art.

To write in a manner where at its root is awareness of oneself and life as a whole brings an entirely different frame of mind that functions with direct observation of reality—of the writer and what is written. To such a person, nothing but the truth can be penned down.

Awareness itself cannot pen down anything as it is not a doing. There is no doing when there is awareness—there is only looking as everything happens—and one has a clear view with no filters or obstructions of any kind.

There is also a power in hand-picking which part of the past to examine deliberately. When there is clarity about what the past is, the individual can carefully and willingly go back, reflect, and take that specific experience to write it down in a way that is unique to them. This applies to what the individual has gone through, which puts them in a special setting wherein they can ponder over the learning and construct their experiences into writing.

This becomes an even more powerful ability if one has interests and curiosity in different areas, which can then be combined however the writer deems necessary. How one writes depends on one's clarity of articulating what is on one's mind, which depends on one's clarity of what the mind is and how its contents end up dictating day-to-day activities, all of one's decisions and life. If this isn't the most important to pay attention to, I have no clue what is.

A writer is someone who can deal with life happenings better than most people, not because he can write about it to overcome pain or as an escape, but because it is very likely that he has lived that experience through his writings already, and the situation more or less seems like the only time he gets to see it happen in front of him.

The words ought to act only as a passage—to signify that which is alive and throbbing in this unending moment. The unending moment is completely different from what the words convey, just as the word sun isn't the sun itself; in the same way, all the words used to describe something that is at the root of existence have no connection with the creator. The human vocabulary is nought when it comes to speaking about the ineffable. Those who realize this deeply become available to grace.

+ Thinking of even one person in your life can be turned into a range of topics and writings.

+ Thinking of their limitations, the way the person lives, and how they can improve their quality of life.

+ Seeing things that one has improved upon for the better can be used as a course for others to improve in that aspect.

+ The problem and solution that *you* know and have experienced can be made universal as all humans face very similar problems, which is not evident to a lot of people and hence struggle.

When one writes about themselves, they add their unique touch, as no two people have the same experiences, skills, and way of writing. This is why books and even content on the internet of the same or similar topics are written by people from all over the world and yet they sell because different people connect with the *style* of how one writes and what they write about.

Off the top of my mind, any person can ponder and go on writing in their own unique ways about literally anything and everything. The random thoughts, the life-changing events, the lessons, the incidents, the memories, the growth, the outlook, the difficulties, the shortcomings, the if onlys, the good, the bad, the ugly, the friends, the family, the relationships, the life purpose, the meanings, the interpretations, the highest point of experience, the rock bottoms, the rejections, the success, the rise and fall, the losses, the gains, the science, the philosophies, the nature, the countries, the world, the planets, the space, the galaxies, the universe, the black holes, the journey, and the existence. You know you are a darn good writer when you can write about anything, anytime, anywhere.

These and many, many more that pique your interest and curiosity can be put into writing as actualities, with fusions, and *in great depth if one consciously pours the words out, not to sell but to express.*

When there is an expression of that which has been wailing to be expressed for a long time, it comes out with a gust of love as that which is unexpressed is constantly working itself out to be expressed. This includes everything in existence. One can see this play clearly when there is awareness of oneself.

It is commonly used in spirituality that when one understands oneself everything else becomes clear. There is truth in it and it has been there throughout to be seen. It is the filters of the mind—the various contents—that obstruct the direct view. The contents of the mind bring in multiple barriers to viewing the reality of what one is and what everything is.

There is only one thing I can do wholeheartedly without the creeps of not knowing enough about a subject, and that is writing. I wish I could write day in and day out and keep birthing life onto paper...

The flow of your writing is in the dance of the words you know and the depth of consciousness you are in touch with. Conscious writing cannot be taught. When I write, I do not exist as an individual.

I write, sitting among the greats who etched on paper their beautiful mind. I do not wish to be one, as it is long past not to be corrupted by modern influences. What I do wish is for one person to read it, to really read it over the course of a few months or even years, as I did with the only scripture I ever read, WALDEN by Henry David Thoreau. I say not at once, as everything about the world now is instant. It is not a movie to be watched and be done with, but the actual life at our hands. Perhaps one day you will understand the world you are born in and the time of it that is not in your control. What is is how you live, for that is all there is.

This is my knowing. If you end up connecting with what I have penned down during my revelation times, I would be amazed because I never met someone with matching perspectives in my vicinity. I would then say—I am glad to finally meet you!

There ought to be a new generation of writers who do not simply wish to sell to the masses. Who will take out the pen with a sense of their presence in the world, humble and aware of those who clean to that which webs; of all who have perished and live in memory; of the incredible trails of the past in the eyes of the present; of all that will be left behind upon what already has been lost.

There are a hundred other things you could have otherwise chosen to be doing. But, you are with this book. You have chosen to read what I have written down when I sat down to write it. In a way, these are the words that have traveled in time for you.

I went to the woods because I wanted to **live deliberately**.
I wanted to live deep and suck out all the marrow of life.
To put to rout all that was not life. And not, when I came to die,
discover that I had not lived
(Thoreau, 1854).

~

Lesson 76 — Pragmatic Spirituality.

Spirituality alone cannot sustain a person's overall development and progress as a human being. Yes, it does provide a perspective that is larger than the individual, but in addition to it, there needs to be an intellectual understanding and grasping of the individual's psychological world created by the mind since childhood.

Often, overlooking what was missing in the child's healthy development leads to misunderstandings of the adult version's way of living as he continues to act out of fear to either fill that void that was missed in childhood or to escape from it.

The combined approach of the perception of spirituality with the understanding of science brings about the balance that one requires to be *able* to live completely without the effects of early life that the child had no control over.

~

Lesson 77 — True Creator.

Content on the internet and amidst all humanity is nothing but the contents of all the works of the innumerable people's mind put together. This is a fact and is quite evident if one is observant. When looked at from one perspective, the knowledge of the entire humanity is the culmination of the mind of individuals who come together to help *you* learn something on a particular day.

How beautiful is that?

There is immense depth in this if one can see it. All of humanity's past and present knowledge come together to *teach* you its contents.

When you realize this fact, not intellectually, but actually realize this fact, there is no undoing it, and you have no choice but to bow down to the true creator who birthed the mind, the humans, and everything else that we can ponder upon.

You are *always* creating as the creator is in you, too!

You are the creator and the creation that goes on creating.

Lesson 78 — A Deep Realization of Reality.

All that we have built is based on reality. The very words we use, too.

The cloud storage is based on the idea of the actual clouds up there, which do not have to be on the ground and which move all over and are seen everywhere.

The words that are used in the business world of humanity are nothing but a form of manipulation to get hold of the masses' unconscious mind that do not have the quality of attention and get lured into anything and everything.

The smartest people in the world have used psychology and the workings of the mind in ways that 99.99% of human beings have no clue about.

That, my friend, is why there are more followers than leaders. The masses are so unconscious that they look up to very few people to *lead* them in every aspect. This ends up creating disparity.

Artificial Intelligence, Machine Learning, and all the so-called inventions are *based* on the human mind and are a replication of it in the human world in order to have a better quality of life. It is beautiful and dangerous.

To put it in another way, *how* the mind operates and *how* we as an individual operate is being translated and reproduced into the automated form of robots and AI in so many forms. But what is usually seen is just the application of it as the luring of information and new technologies is enough for the unconscious-minded people to get hooked to the very things that they themselves have in the form of the mind.

In a sense, *the mind has created an external reality of its own for people to dig themselves ever further to remain and live in the contents of the mind.*

When it becomes obvious to a person that *all* that we as humans have created is a *copy* of the nature that we see on the outside and what we are within us, that puts an end to all the luring of the modern corrupted world.

After such a deep, deliberate observation, there is no turning back for that person as he has seen the reality of the world, and even if he indulges in such activities, the consciousness will continue to spread within the realms of all that is unconscious within him.

This is the power of consciousness.

Once there is a looking of the unconscious—a deep awareness that we have lived so unconsciously for decades—the consciousness *seeps* into the contents of the mind for all that is being done unconsciously.

When such a process begins, there is no stopping it as the person has touched the deepest part of his own creation, which is the creator that is no different than the creation.

This is not an understanding that takes place with the mind but a deep realization and awareness of the reality itself, which is indivisible and whole.

~

Lesson 79 — Flow of Purpose: Align With Your Innate Skills.

You can help another person with what you already know. That is more than enough.

Yes, there is so much more to know, and there always will be. But that doesn't mean you withdraw from helping because you want it to be at a perfect time when you have everything.

Just a conversation with a stranger can spark the wisdom that you already do have. For that, you need to be open to receiving the way others are, too, the way they think. When you connect with a person on the same level of enthusiasm and understanding, there is an innate curiousness that comes alive from beneath that has not been paid much attention amongst the thousand other habitual things. This curiousness and aliveness is a path that keeps showing up every now and then, and if you can catch the significance of what it means for you— what you are genuinely capable and naturally skilled in, comes to the surface for you to see.

The more times this happens, the more it grows in you to move toward your natural skills, which are not learned but innate. It is that subtle power that you have that can blow out of proportion if you pay enough attention to it. That power is what one day will drive you to do the things you really wish to and get in sync with your life's purpose.

I say purpose singularly because there cannot be depth if we assign ourselves a number of purposes, which then spreads out the attention we give to each. That one purpose, when you align with it, is enough on its own to last a lifetime, and even a lifetime looks short.

Time, as we know it, flies when you are in sync with your purpose.

This innate ability will keep showing up for you to see. It won't go away. It is like a child that hasn't been paid attention to and keeps demanding it.

Why you are stuck is because you haven't been paying any attention to that child in the form of your natural strengths and skills.

You. Already. Have it.

You already know what it is. It is not something you will find by absorbing more information from the outside but something that will rise up to your consciousness when you sit with yourself and look at yourself with complete honesty. There may be things to learn to put that into practice, but first, you got to observe it within yourself as to what it is.

For me, that innate ability was writing.

It took me 33 years to realize—a rather simple fact—that this is my natural ability where the flow is for me. It was naturally there during my college days to make detail-oriented notes, and I wouldn't start studying until the notes of all the topics in the subject were done with first. Writing at that time was in the form of organizing information that was already there in the subjects. Do that for 5 years deeply, and you become really good at organizing and puzzling chaotic things together. This skill then allowed me to permeate organization into other areas of my life, including the mind itself. Having a problem at hand and putting my imaginary formless hat on to lay down all the possible routes to go about solving it and picking out the best possible option among the laid-out routes became second hand to me by the time I started my first job as a Researcher. At that time, I was not even aware of such a gift, but I was already utilizing it. Coincidentally, my work involved testing out a lot of open-source tools to pick the best, which, again, was my natural strength. I loved doing just that since it involved feeding in a lot of random information from the scientific papers, but as I was adept at organizing spread out information, spending time over researching or picking the best out of 100s of tools happened on its own without me working for it. In hindsight, those years of preparing notes for the exams turned me into an organization machine, and this helped me put together and make sense of the work, the environment, and relationships as well.

There is chaos in the form of information in the mind, and when you see that there is chaos and dive each time into looking at how randomly the information keeps playing out in the form of thoughts and memories, in that very act of conscious looking, two things happen—either the organization takes place if that information is useful or there is an ending to that stream of information that plays out compulsively. *That is the power of looking with awareness.*

For work purposes, we end up organizing a ton of information without being aware and fare well. One can imagine the possibilities and limitless potential that exist when *awareness* comes into play. This is by no means an exaggeration, but I have witnessed the evolution in the quality of my writing from what it was in 2007 to what it is today, as awareness keeps taking root in everything it touches and lays eyes on.

There tends to be no order in which the mind stores the information, as randomness is at the core of existence. The mind behaves no differently than the existence. Just like it takes effort to organize physically and takes no effort at all for the untouched places to turn messy, the unconscious, or so to say the *unobserved* or *unlooked* part of the mind, is chaotic by default as the mind has taken its paradoxically designed task of organizing its contents with the randomness of what it knew best at that time of experiencing. There is no order in how the mind stores such content. The paradox is that its design is to organize and categorize all of its stored content. But because there is no order in the first place, all the information is unconsciously categorized according to the psychological value we hold for them, according to the meanings that are assigned to each and every information. And because the mind has evolved with survival as its foundation, its survival instincts do not go away and it seeps in at the time when it is creating order and structure out of randomness to *fulfill* its functionality. Hence the paradox of structure with randomness in the mind.

To bring it all together, the mind, by default, has no order, but because of its paradoxical existence, it ends up creating order out of the randomness that it itself has created. It may sound like the mind is a closed system, but it is not. *The mind is what connects our limited human experiences with that which doesn't even exist. It acts as a link to* **Nilness,** *but it is not a bridge that can be crossed over to find something because there is nothing to be found where nothing exists.*

The last two words can either be interpreted as one—nothing exists—or two—but *nothing* does *exist*—and this, my dear friend, is exactly how the mind divides each and everything it touches into two unless it is bathed with *awareness* and the unmet needs of the child are fulfilled by paying attention to your innate ability and natural skills.

The mind is the closest entity, if I may use that word, to the creator itself.
The one that is still.
The one that is immovable but is responsible for all the dance that we see.

If this is read with depth and awareness and linked to our everyday life, this itself is enough to work on oneself for a lifetime. That is the power of awareness and freedom.

The existence, too, has order and structure with randomness.
The mind is the same as the rest of existence in its *deepest* essence, and so are you.

~

Lesson 80 — The Golden Lighthouse.

Strength of natural strengths:

Knowing what your strengths are, be it quality-wise or skill-wise, puts you in charge of situations as they arise.

+ Sit on your own in a quiet place with a pen and paper. Write down what are the things that naturally come to you without feeling like it is an effort. It could be talking, reading, helping others, driving, swimming, climbing, questioning, finding solutions, writing, or anything. Even the smallest of things, such as keeping your place clean and tidy, giving your best at work, and being calm in difficult situations.

+ Accept what others do in their life. Their problems are—not your problems to solve. You yourself have enough to see and undo.

To speak broadly, being swayed by the activities of others and reacting to every little thing is what causes restlessness within you. I know it is not easy to implement in real-life situations where you are expected to handle the situation in a calm manner.

Maybe you will go through all the difficult times.
Maybe the difficult times are there to show you that there are deeper issues for you to resolve and grow in.
Maybe the most grievous situations you have been in have been repeated several times in your life to show you that the same way of dealing with it is not going to work at all and requires a different perspective to go about handling the problem.
Maybe all you can do is—let it be.

Come to terms with the psychological problems that you have, those you very well know you have them. There is nothing to be ashamed about *looking* at your own patterns of how you go about everyday situations, other people, what you think, what you hold on to, and how you try to *fill* in this void of not looking —with control. Control is never going to work. There is nothing to be controlled. Just let yourself be. Let other people in your life be, too. And then allow the flow of life to do its charm without any effort, and all you have to do is be there and witness it unfold in front of you.

What you do not like in others is exactly what you need to work on within yourself.

This is a golden lighthouse that is always there to *show* you what to work on. If one is able to grasp the intensity of how often and how efficiently the golden lighthouse works for us, it would baffle them. It never stops to show us where the problems lie within ourselves. The golden lighthouse is *untouched* by— our emotions and how we end up responding or reacting to the outside and the inside. The golden lighthouse is a signal to convey the information of what a human needs to *undo* by looking at it. The golden lighthouse acts as a gateway for an unconscious person to light up the darkness that is holding us back from being in touch with the **Nilness**.

All it takes is very simple. Question and look. When you dislike something about yourself or another person:

+ Question yourself, "What is it that you are not liking?"

+ See, "Why you don't like it?"

+ Look deeper. "What is the first memory of this dislike?"

When you keep *questioning* your dislikes and pay *attention* to what comes up, it acts as a light upon your darkness. Lighting up your dislikes is what will bring it to the surface for you to see and drop it completely. The same can be done with the likings, too and drop them psychologically. There is nothing to end physically. There is no actual danger other than the made-up fears of the mind.

All the likes act as a form of attachment, too. This is not about *not doing* what we like in the physical world but more about not putting it up at such a level where we hold it as the *only* way. There is no absolute way for anything. We have our skills with which we earn money to spend on what we want. There is nothing more to it than that. But in the modern world, the work is made to look like it is the only aspect to focus on and dedicate your life to. No, it is *one* of the aspects. There are more things in life than what you work on solely for money.

While you drop the likes and dislikes internally, you can also make working effortless by creating a new way of living for yourself. One where all your natural strengths come into play. One where these very strengths can be put into action by designing a particular way of living with the core of it involving your strengths. This will change the course of your lifetime drastically as you will be in sync with your natural skills along with a means of earning a living by implementing your strengths out into the world, thereby expressing your true self.

~

Lesson 81 — Contents of the Mind.

Figuring out what the mind is cannot be done by being amongst the contents of the mind.

One needs to either zoom out to see its externalities—which is superficial, still showing all of its contents albeit a bigger picture —or zoom in to see the root or source of the contents of the mind, which is of the deepest level to perceive that everything *is* in the ever-flowing unending moment.

There is no end to the contents of the mind.

One can go on living in it without knowing what death is, or one can learn **The Art of Eliminating** and ending on a daily basis to come to a point where death becomes a living reality.

What has happened is already done.
You don't need to repeat them to keep them alive as the mind is potent enough to do that, and it is very efficient at it.

One must have **The Art of Sensitivity** to perceive what *is* in reality. If one is not sensitive, the body, which is the means through which the physical reality is sensed, is itself turned off, which completely blocks perceiving anything other than living in the contents of the mind. The sensitivity of the body and the senses as a whole is the foundation on which the oneness of existence can be realized.

A realization of everything—what is within and what is on the outside is together, is one, is whole.

One must learn **The Art of Being Here** without all the burden of memories. To just be in this ever-lasting, unending moment in its entirety.

One needs to balance the systemization to live on a daily basis with **The Art of Nilness**, to live in a reality where the mind is never a problem.

There are others who love what you hate.

There are others who hate what you love.
These are the limitations of the mind.
There is literally *nothing* to be hated or loved in reality.

It is our *experience* in relation to that *thing* that makes us become extreme about it. See the things you have conditionings in and work your way out of it.

Mind is a constant flux of endless variations. See the fact of the mind, for how dangerous it is to *let* its contents *drive* your everyday life. You are not in charge, but the contents of the mind are. It's not you consciously living but moving as per the movements of the contents of the mind.

Where is freedom in this? Isn't this the worst form of slavery, where the mind dictates you to live based on its contents?

There are no layers in the mind. Layers and parts of the mind are named for understanding purposes *only*—to understand the various depths. The more any information is repeated, the deeper the information and the processing of it is in the mind. Without awareness, this deeply stored information that a person has no access to takes the role in the background of the individual's daily activities, thinking, actions, behavior, patterns, and all the facets of how the person's mind works, which in turn *dictates* his moment-to-moment quality of life.

Sticking to words and the meanings we give to them is a trap of a lifetime if one doesn't see the limitations of human language in how epically short it falls flat on its face to even begin to describe the truth or the reality. When we assign meanings to the information given through words, we may end up using that meaning as a mechanism, as if that assigned meaning is the only way.

Yes, the meanings did help you get through a rough phase in life and difficult times.
Yes, the meanings do help you deal with people and society.
Yes, it is human nature to create meanings out of our experiences.

Yes, you do require a meaning and framework to live sustainably in the world.

But that's about it. *When the work of the meaning assigned to that information is done, you can simply drop that meaning when it's not in use.* Will you do this? Or you can hold on to that meaning, build up a structure, and let the mind construct a world of its own, which would become so difficult to see it's not real in the first place since it has been artificially constructed. And if one cannot even see that it's not real, there is no chance in heaven or hell that they would ever perceive anything more than the contents of the mind.

If this doesn't instill the danger of seeing the world and yourself through the filters created by the mind and an urgent necessity to see something apart from the contents of the mind, I don't know what will.

The voice that you hear and has no place to point to, is yours and not yours.

The mind consists of the following. This is not to show that there are categories in the mind which are again interpreted and understood as different things, but rather to depict the contents of the mind just as the chapters in a book show what the book has in store for you to read:

+ Voices of other people.

+ Your voice or you talking to yourself.

+ You conversing with another person.

+ Random information.

+ Repetition of information, meanings, and patterns.

+ Sound.

That's it. This is all there is in all the activities of the mind.

+ Eliminate other people's voices to hear your own.

+ Notice what you talk to yourself or others.

+ When something pops up randomly, be it a song, a dialogue from movies, or whatever else that is *not worth paying attention to*, let it play out till the end.

The ending of it is where true freedom is. Let it play, and as you observe without looking at yourself as an observer, the one that is observing and the one that is observed—in this case, the thoughts playing themselves out—are one and the same.

What is observing and what is being observed are not separate.

It takes sheer conscious looking to see such a union that will lovingly destroy the mind's compulsion to come in between you and the reality that is not separate, where there is no division.

The mind is not a problem, but its function is to divide, and it does its job in the most efficient manner. But once you see that the observer and the observed are not separate, the mind falls into its right place where as a human being, you can use the mind and all of its contents whenever you require, whenever you need to.

The compulsiveness of the contents of the mind playing out all the time comes to an end, and this, too, is not an event or a happening.

It is just a realization.

~

Lesson 82 — The Mind of Humanity.

The whole relation with what the mind is has been divided into a thousand different ways.

First, let's begin with the body:

We have numerous medical specialties when it comes to the body.

Anaesthesiology | Cardiology | Dermatology | Endocrinology | Gastroenterology | General Practice/Family Medicine | Geriatrics | Gynaecology | Haematology | Hepatology | Infectious Diseases | Internal Medicine | Laryngology | Medical Genetics | Nephrology | Neurology | Neurosurgery | Obstetrics | Oncology | Ophthalmology | Orthopaedic Surgery | Otology | Otorhinolaryngology (ENT) | Pathology | Paediatrics | Plastic Surgery | Podiatry | Preventive Medicine | Proctology | Psychiatry | Pulmonology | Radiology | Radiation Oncology | Reproductive Medicine | Rheumatology | Sports Medicine | Surgery (General) | Thoracic Surgery | Urology | Vascular Surgery

Do you see the problem here?

We surely do need experts for medical treatment. Without them, there would have been no improvement in the quality and time of our lifespan. But, the problem I am trying to get to here is that when one actually lives in such a way where they see their own body parts as divided and live with the names of it and not with the body itself, there is a dire issue of living with the very words that we use and not with the reality of the body. We do require words to convey to another person or even to ourselves at various times, but one must also have *the freedom to look at their hand and not think of the word hand in any manner.*

+ Freedom to move as a whole body and not just the legs.

+ Freedom to hear, see, smell, touch, eat, and not make them into separate happenings that are independent on their own.

+ All of your body is together.

+ All of your body is alive and functioning together.

+ All of your senses erupt with sensations at the same time. You don't first hear, then see, then smell, then feel, and then munch. It is all happening at the same instant. At once. Never apart.

Coming back to the mind, how can one truly relate to the mind as one when the very words we use to make ourselves and other people understand are divided? In the very effort to understand *that* which is not physical in its nature, we have ended up splitting the mind into so many aspects. This is because it is *still the mind gathering all the information to understand what its own nature is.*
Do you see how absurd such an approach is?

One can never see what the mind is as a whole when it itself is operating to understand itself by being inside all of its contents.

Science is pure analysis. It is not a direct observation of the mind. Science has its place and purpose. But it has no place in the direct perception of the mind itself, as it is designed to work with data—a result of the mind—and the contents of the mind are what one cannot afford in order to have a direct perception of the truth.
The analysis has its place too. But the understanding through these very analyses is what confuses everybody and obstructs having a clear view of reality.

Take the words we use for the mind:

Consciousness | thought | idea | concept | memory | emotion | feeling | belief | opinion | perspective | perception | cognition | intellect | reasoning | logic | intuition | insight | imagination | fantasy | dream | vision | awareness | attention | focus | concentration | contemplation | reflection | meditation | knowledge | understanding | wisdom | psyche | subconscious | unconscious | ego | superego | id | mental state | mindset | outlook

| attitude | disposition | temperament | mood | will | desire | wish | aspiration | motivation | drive | impulse | instinct | mental image | recollection | remembrance | recall | recognition | learning | sense | sensation | realization | comprehension | discernment | judgment | decision | choice | intent | intention | purpose | goal | objective | aim | plan | strategy | tactic | thought process | stream of consciousness | thoughtlessness | oblivion | forgetfulness | amnesia | mindlessness | mindfulness | mental health | mental illness | neurosis | psychosis | delusion | hallucination | illusion | daydream | nightmare | fixation | obsession | compulsion | phobia | mania | depression | anxiety | stress | worry | fear | hope | faith | trust | doubt | skepticism | curiosity | wonder | amazement | surprise | shock | bewilderment | confusion | disorientation | clarity | lucidity | coherence | self-awareness | presence | here-and-now | experience | expertise | skill | talent | ability | capability | competence | proficiency | aptitude | faculty | capacity | potential | possibility | opportunity | introspection | affect | self | persona | archetype | metacognition | flow | love | hate | empathy | sympathy | compassion | mind | brain | neural | psychology | psychiatry | psychoanalysis | behaviourism | existential | humanistic | psychodynamic | psychotherapy | neuropsychology

Do you see the problem here?

As with the body, we have used the same approach and divided the understanding of the mind, be it for coping with it, treatments, or improving day-to-day life.

All these words have made millions and billions of people *live* in the world of these words.
How surreal is that?

When one sees how much of an impact this has had in truly relating to the mind and why there is so much chaos in the human world, the *root* of the problem comes to the attachment to the words we use. It may seem silly, but people *literally live in these very words*. They make it into a grand thing and live or die for these words.

In reality, these words are nothing but the constructs of the mind itself. But when *intense meanings and significance* are given to any of the words, that turns into a made-up reality for that person or the community of people or a state or a group or a country, which is nothing but a grand *illusion*.

The only solution is to see the mind as *one*. This does not mean getting rid of the words we require to live in this world but rather a different approach to relate to the mind that each of the 8.2 billion human beings experiences.

+ It is not your mind.

+ It is not my mind.

+ It is **The Mind of Humanity** that you experience.

That mind is one, irrespective of whether you ever realize that or not. This mind operates as one *with* existence and not separate from it.

If I may, it is also a fact that this is **The Mind of Humanity** that ever existed.

It is the mind of 117 billion people who have ever walked this planet.

This statement can never be proved by science, but it is a fact that the mind that we have today has been shaped by the immense history of all the humans who have ever lived.

There is so much disorder in the world today because there is disorder in the collective human mind consciousness. This brings us to a very important point where—for things to change from hereafter, there is an urgent need for a shift in the imbalance of human consciousness. There is no other way out of all the problems the mind has created in the world by dividing each and everything it touches.

Such a shift to bring in some sort of balance in the world mandates people like you and me to realize the truth and directly see the reality of existence—**The Oneness of Existence**.

Nobody else can do it for you.

Only you can merge with the rest of existence, soak in the immensity of it, and turn yourself into a beacon of light for the rest of humanity.

Lesson 83 — It is Nilness.

It is a paradox of thinking, knowing, and understanding, which can be completely different from what the reality is. What I mention here goes against all of science because it is coming from a place of truth, and the interpretations of the mind has no place in reality.

Disclaimer: Put a hat hereafter that is devoid of any contents of the mind. Are you ready? Here we go.

*Sound can exist only in a vacuum of something, and by vacuum, I mean emptiness or, as I like to call it—***Nilness**. We see space as something beyond Earth, but there is space right around you. The very space that holds your body and existence. You are alive right now because there is a symbiotic space that allows you to co-habitat the environment of the planet. But how many people have you seen even talk about this space? This is why it becomes a necessity to talk about the reality of how things are instead of living in the makings of what the mind thinks the reality is.

A space that talks about everything outside the human mind. Nothing of the interpretations of the mind as is usually done, but words that are reality themselves without an iota of *me* as the center, without an iota of everything else is around me, for me, for the human I am, for the species we are.
This is not reality.
Reality *just is*.
Reality or the truth is without any language.

Hence, the human language falls flat to describe what reality is, but the paradox of life is that words are the only way a human can express even the deepest of experiences and perceptions. Which is why we write down words, read them, utter them, and use them to talk with another, and is the basis of information as we know it. The poets use it in their own way, the artists use the imaginary version of the words, the writer uses the very words along with reflection and projection of his memories, and in

223

millions of other ways, the language of words is used by us.

What people don't really pay close attention to is that *the words are arising out of the memories that the mind has stored ever since you came into this world.* The words are a result of the stored language and information. There is no other way one can use words without knowing them in the first place.

How did you come to know about the words that you speak and think in?
From the people who brought you up to the influences of each and every person you have come across, the language you think and speak is based on it.

Where did these people know of these words before you came into this world?
From their set of people they were brought up in, and this goes back and back and back to an era which was a pre-human existence to a time which would be—*the first sound of Earth.* It was not by any organism as we know it, but there was a first sound that our Mother Earth made billions of years ago. *That* sound was in a different form than what the human senses can fathom. That is the beginning of sound in the **Nilness** that we live in.

That is where everything in this **Nilness** we live in began, and to this day, the **Nilness** exists and is the true foundation of what we see on this planet. The very basis of the planet's existence is **Nilness**. Without it, it wouldn't have come into existence or anything else for that matter. Even the words created by humans, which are nothing but sound—arise out of the **Nilness** in which the memories are held. The very memories that are held in what we call the mind exists because there is **Nilness**. It is what is holding this body together, too.

Without the vacuum or emptiness or the **Nilness**, there is not a single entity that can exist.

You see, sound requires a vacuum to exist and to come into existence. Everything has rooting in the **Nilness** to be in existence. Sound arises *out* of **Nilness**. Thought is a sound and it arises out of the vacuum, which is the very reason we cannot ever pinpoint a location of where the thoughts are because there is no place to point to it. It doesn't exist.

We will never find out what **Nilness** is because it cannot be found. It is just there. Out of which everything exists—from the smallest to the largest and nothing can exist without it.

This is the God all religions are praying to. This is the dark matter that science wants to find out, but they can't as it doesn't exist. Science will find and master everything around it, but never *it*. Science is always going to be about the resultants, the creation, the products but never the creator itself.

This *human body that you have is a reverberation of sound itself!* This fact cannot be understood by the mind but has to be perceived beyond the senses to get the immensity of it.
You, in this human form, are a vacuum for the sound of thoughts. Without this, you can't have a thinking different from others. Read that again. *You are a vacuum for the sound of thoughts.*

A single thought that arises is a sound. That sound exists because there is a vacuum. The bigger vacuum is our planet, but for you to experience all that you do as a human being, to experience yourself as an individual human being, there is a range of vacuums for a zillion different things to keep you together.

The human body is that vacuum that paves the way for the human mind to exist and for you to think on your own, but it is not separate from **The Mind of Humanity**. **The Mind of Humanity** exists as an entire entity, as a whole, and not as 8.2 billion separate minds who live today. It cannot be. It isn't.

The illusion of having a separate mind has arrived because of the individuality of experiencing life as a human being with separate bodies. We indeed have separate bodies, but that is the result of the progression of the species that we are.

If there was not a single human being other than you, would you even know that you are a separate individual? Since we visually see and mentally experience the drastic differences in how I am or how I even think, is so not aligned with how another person thinks or behaves; over time, we tend to build up a wall of *this is me,* and *that is them.*

The mind has a billion different ways to keep itself secure, and this has been engraved in **The Mind of Humanity** due to the survival days of humanity. But the mind is such that it *cannot* be free of the contents of humanity, and its nature is such that it persists with being influenced by all that humanity has ever witnessed.

Nothing has and ever will be forgotten in **The Mind of Humanity** till the last human being exists.

The individual human experience of 8.2 billion people *is* **The Mind of Humanity** which is also shaped by a total of 117 billion people in totality. This has continued with every generation of people that have been born and has contents from not only since the beginning of our species but traces of existence that are present within **The Mind of Humanity** goes back to the first rupture out of **Nilness**—*the very first time the existence came into being. All* that is in you, right now, this second.

Is there anything more beautiful than that, that you get to experience all of existence within the minuscule that you are in this existence?

There is nothing grander than this. It needs subtlety in the purest of form for a human to experience and perceive this grandness. Otherwise it only becomes a topic of talking and nothing else. It cannot be talked about or thought of.

The magnificence of a human being is in making use of the human limitation to see the reality of existence and that which doesn't exist too—the **Nilness**.

Only one who has truly realized and gone into the depths of who he is can see all this without an iota of the mind in that minuscule faster-than-light moment that is a million times smaller than the Planck Time. That minuscule, faster-than-light moment that is a million times smaller than Planck Time is exactly what enlightens a human into a being, and it becomes a part of his perception permanently.

That is what *enlightenment* is all about.

Mind is never a problem after that as it falls into its right place and nothing more than that.

Enlightenment is perceiving a moment so deeply and wholly that there is nothing to compare it with as the *other* disintegrates.

Laws of physics do not exist here.

Laws of humanity cannot exist here.

The existence of words and the mind itself as a separate entity falls apart in that minuscule, faster-than-light moment.

It is perceiving the silence *at the end of a thought.*

Here is where *timelessness* is for a human being.

~

Lesson 84 — Enlightenment: The Overlooked Simplicity.

There is a straightforward way to spiritual awakening. The universe's secrets are unraveled not through complex machinery or quantum equations but through the simple act of observing.

Leaves rustling, clouds drifting—these aren't just background scenery but an invitation for us to get out of compulsive thinking and observe.

Focusing intensely on these natural phenomena can allow one to dive into the depths of one's consciousness. It is like trying to find the ultimate pixel of existence—the smallest point in time and space where everything just... clicks.

Go *deeper and deeper* into observation until you reach an *intraword pause* at the level down to *one thought*. Let me also throw in Planck's Time—but a million times smaller.

You are not just looking to observe; you're aiming to become one with the infinitesimal, to experience a moment so brief, it's almost non-existent. It is non-existent.

This deep observation leads to a realization, a moment of profound understanding where time itself seems irrelevant. It is a *deep* observation in which the observer, the observee, and the act of observing become one.

Enlightenment comes not from grand, life-altering experiences but from the quiet, persistent contemplation of simplicity. Any tree or the passing clouds are potential hotspots for enlightenment—which is just what humanity needs now. It is very much a possibility for any human being.

Enlightenment is a subtle realization devoid of any dramatic breakthrough moment.

Although it is the most subtle realization a human being can have, it has been made to look like a big thing, and the mind clings on to it to be a big thing, making a person miss the whole point. Do not go on reading about how another person might have gotten enlightened. It is not true to you anyway.

Even if you read such a thing, have an atomic garbage to throw that information in. One should have atomic garbage for any information, for that matter, as the mind remembers all the things you put into it anyway, and there is no need for you to remember anything by effort.

There is no grand *ah-ha* moment of when the enlightenment happens. Enlightenment doesn't even need a moment as it takes place in this unending moment in which there is no this or that moment. It just is.

Enlightenment is just another deep realization, the only difference being—that there is no iota of the mind's contents in that moment of realization of the unending moment of reality. The mind is never a problem after that. It is as if putting a person at the extreme of a *phase transition point* wherein he undergoes a significant change not by an external force but by his own *deliberate deep observation*.

Enlightenment is as simple as tree watching—it may sound poetic, but *it is the simplest explanations that often turn out to be the right ones*. For a person to be simple these days, the things they need to keep themselves away from are a challenge. But if you are somebody who likes simplicity, go ahead.

In essence, by observing nature, one can achieve a state of awareness so intense that it transcends normal perception, leading to a moment of realization that's both incredibly brief and profoundly deep. It's like trying to understand a universe inside an atom or perhaps understanding the entirety of human existence through the movement of a single leaf.

Keep staring at those leaves, my friend. You might just catch the existence blinking back to let you see the oneness that is staring right at all the 8.2 Billion people.

ANIL KANTHI

~

Lesson 85 — Returning to the Source: The Root of All Yearnings.

There is a deep yearning in each one of us to keep going back.

We go back when we think, reflect, and ponder over our memories. We go back in time, away from the present unending moment, to be in those memories in order to keep reliving them.

We keep going back to the addictions of the mind, and this could be anything ranging from excessive cleaning to binge-watching movies to being in back-to-back relationships.

There is a deep need to *want* to have what was before. Once there is an experience of what has been before, we want it again. There is a sense of temporary settlement when we do get that need fulfilled. But it does not last long. In that very need being fulfilled, there is also a yearning for something more.

This yearning for something more takes shape in the form of:

Money, love, happiness, sexuality, material wealth, health, knowledge, success, power, recognition, time, freedom, security, comfort, experiences, friendships, creativity, peace, adventure, beauty, wisdom, and fulfillment.

Partaking in any of these is not a problem. But if one realizes that the root of all their yearnings is fundamentally coming from a call to realize the true nature of existence. When one deeply sees this realization as the most important, there begins a spiritual journey that lasts for years, decades, and a lifetime. I say a lifetime since you are in this human form, and there is no escaping from all that it comes with.

All the people before us who awakened to the true nature of reality also had to face the reality of their physical death. Nothing can escape death as the rise and fall is the design of existence. Similarly, once you are born as a human being, you come with a deep calling to return to the source. The source that you are. The source that is within and all around you.

The source itself does not exist. I have used the word **Nilness** for it, but it is basically devoid of anything. It does not exist but is the source behind all existence. Usually, the word *source* is taken as a point from which something emerges. But the source that is **Nilness** is not a point and cannot be pointed at because what doesn't exist cannot be pointed out.

Though **Nilness** does not exist, it can be realized and lived with. This is another paradox of life where something can be touched and come back from, back and forth, effortlessly. *That* is the power of choice that a human being gets once he sees the non-duality of existence. The choice to effortlessly get back in touch with **Nilness** and live with it in everyday life. This is the God you and the rest of the religious and spiritual folks have been looking for for eons.

The source of all creation is **Nilness**. Getting back in touch with your true creator and existing with it is the only purpose of a human being that matters the most. Once you touch this sacred space, the mind still functions, but now it knows its right place in front of the creator and does not behave as if it is the creator.

~

Lesson 86 — The Art of Being.

An entire army will stand in front of you to stop you from getting in sync with the natural flow of life. The army includes the mind that you experience and of the others. This is the main barrier to seeing reality for what it is, to see the truth of life, the entire existence, and that which doesn't exist.

An army of hurdles in the form of people, difficulties, regrets, past, inadequacy, unfulfillment, desires, traumas, identities, memories, losses, physical sickness, mindset, experiences, attachments, and in various other ways will and have to stand in front of you when the journey of revealing that truth of your existence in the human form has begun.

The truth shows itself up and can *only* show itself up to those who defeat each and everything that is not allowing them to look at the truth because:

The truth put itself into motion—to exist—and is eternally in a flow of getting back to itself.

That is **Nilness**.

+ That which put itself into motion is the force of creation itself.

+ That which is unmoved.

+ That which has always been unmoved *but* moves everything, itself being static.

+ That which is spread out in everything that is physical but remains hidden.

+ That which is with no sound.

+ That which has no actuality.

+ That which is at the core of everything a human ever experiences.

+ That which experiences.

+ That which was never born.

+ That which can never die.

+ That which put into motion a journey back to itself.

That which a human being perceives to be enlightened and returns to share it with the world. Because he cannot help but let others know that all the sufferings we as humans impose on ourselves and this wonderful world are baseless. To share that all of our sufferings are utterly avoidable *if* and only *if* we could *imbibe* the reality of existence.

A play of being here in the form of humans and not being here. Here is where the truth reveals itself.

It is as simple as that.

You do not need to do anything. If you do something to see the reality, it's gone because that is your doing as a human. The reality is not a doing of whatsoever proportions. It is just there.

When an entity in the form of a human deeply sees that—what is looking at the creation is the creator itself, a rapture of the highest possible state as a human being takes place.

When a human deeply absorbs **The Art of Being** with the creator's unending moment, that is **The Art of Nilness**.

Lesson 87 — Prepare To Die.

Having an outlook where one keeps questioning about death brings one closer and closer to **The Art of Eliminating** death itself as a fear.

Death is nothing but a fear of not knowing what death is. If you see that death is nothing but an ending of who you are, then it becomes really clear. The next question that arises is, "Who am I?"

If this body can die, does that mean that you will also die? Do you die when you sleep? Are you aware of your surroundings when you sleep? There is an ending right there. As you lay asleep, what you are when you are awake has ended and isn't alive anymore as you sleep.

When you take the breath in, there is a feeling of being full as the lungs fill up and are filled with the air that you take in. When you breathe out, there is an emptying of the air that was inside you and the lungs feel empty. As the breath draws out of you, that is death. The next breath that you take in is what keeps you alive and that is life.

Life and death are happening based on what form you are in. Since you experience this life as a human being, the body that you come with is packed with life and death all over it—including the mind.

All you have to do is become aware and observe the subtleties of the body and the mind.

When your eyes are open, you are awake, and when they are closed, you are closed to what you see. You are closed to see what you can physically see, but you can still be aware deeply.

When it comes to the mind, the rise and fall of thoughts are one of the most beautiful creations that a human can become aware of. You, as a human being, are what births the thoughts. The thoughts do not happen on their own. A single thought requires energy to come forth into creation, and the beauty of all this is that—you, as the creation of the creator, have the capability to create and give rise to thoughts and see them fall into **Nilness**.

A thought is born, and that thought dies into the void of **Nilness**. *The ending of a thought is death.*

If one can purely observe and slowly birth a thought, seeing all the formlessness, speed, and reality of the sound that arises and dies—that is dying. If you can see the ending of a thought so subtly, death becomes as clear as the sky because *death is no different than the ending of a thought.*

At the end of a thought, there is death. When you see this deeply, you will have no more questions about life or death or spirituality or life or anything for that matter.

The fear of dying physically or the thoughts of a loved one dying falls apart after one sees the oneness of reality that is timeless, where nothing can die. It is just as simple as the physical creation that ran out of time physically.

With the realization of the non-duality of life, of reality and the mind, one lives and dies in this unending moment of reality where the mind is never an issue.

When you see the ending of a thought and fall down along with the fall of a thought into the void of Nilness, that is— ending.
That is—death.
That is—enlightenment.
That is—seeing the oneness of reality where the mind falls out of its compulsiveness and converges with the timeless reality.

~

Lesson 88 — The Nil Mind.

Throughout the book, I have emphasized on seeing the mind and the reality as it is. I also do understand that this is not as easy as it sounds.

+ If a person has a child to take care of and is a single parent, he or she would not have much time to give for themselves. A lot of the time would go towards the child. Handling the finances, emotions, and time would be of priority.

+ If a person has problems financially or struggling with the loss of a job and making ends meet to just cover the basic expenses of living, life can really be hard every day.

+ If a person has health issues, either themselves or someone in their family, a lot of the time and energy can go into it.

+ If a person is grieving the loss of a loved one or a close friend, there is a sense of loss that cannot be spoken about.

+ If a person is going through a relationship breakup, emotional or even financial stability is affected.

+ If a person is recovering from an earthquake, hurricane, or flood, they may be left with no home and possessions. Dealing with the loss of a loved one in such a calamity is even harder.

+ If a person is dealing with anxiety, depression, or any other mental health issues, it can be an overwhelming feeling.

+ If a person has elderly parents to take care of, it can take a toll on them physically, financially, and mentally.

These and many many more life situations where, for you, it may not even be on the list to observe the mind, reality, or seek out to find the truth of life. It all seems meaningless to pursue such a thing because there are other more important aspects to deal with that are more urgent.

With all due respect, what I would like to say is—no matter what you are going through, no matter where you are in life, no matter what you have gone through, no matter the number of things you have to do on a day-to-day basis, no matter whether you are rich or poor—there is a part of you that seeks depth.

That which seeks is timeless. The human challenges have nothing to do with seeking to return to the creator. The very situation and the suffering you are in could be the foundation on which you can build the perception to see the truth of life. All the life situations we face are indeed challenging. But when looked at from a different perspective, these hardships could become the groundwork to seek what this life is all about.

The human sufferings are there for a reason. They are there as there is room for growth. Throughout our lives, there are situations we face. When we look back, we see how much those very hardships made us grow as a person. The choices that we make are what determine how deeply we grow or whether we choose to grow at all.

In the midst of all these sufferings, we as a human being will be able to handle all that life throws at us with greater stability if one is aware of the mind and there is a perception of things as they are and not what the mind wants them to be.

If one can take the clarity of what is mentioned in the book and look at life from a perspective that has simplicity in everything, this simplicity is enough to unravel deep perceptions of life.

+ Observe the mind for what it is.

+ Se the thoughts as they rise and fall.

+ Be completely attentive to the thoughts that happen in the mind.

+ Question each and everything.

+ See the fears for what they are.

+ See all the illusions of the mind.

+ End as much as you can psychologically.

+ Be humble.

+ Craft out a life where your natural qualities and the work that you do align. It doesn't matter how long it takes.

+ Learn and inculcate **The Art of Eliminating, The Art of Sensitivity, The Art of Being Here**, and **The Art of Nilness** in the unending present moment.

All this would bring you to a place where the mind is closer and closer to being nil—empty—whenever you want it to be.

The mind that is nil in the unending moment is the highest form of existing as a human being. It is not something that can be done. It cannot be done as action.

To have a nil mind is an inner work you *must* do.

To look at reality with the mind that is totally empty. That is some way to be. A way that allows you to see the reality of everybody and everything, including life itself.

There is no shortcut to come to **The Nil Mind**. One cannot jump into it without deeply looking at oneself. **The Nil Mind** is empty of all information and yet you have access to all of its information. How can that be possible? Just like the middle of an ocean that appears undisturbed, reflecting only the sky above, **The Nil Mind** is devoid of all of its contents. There is no activity going on, but all the information is there underneath. Just as the depth of the ocean has a water content of unimaginable proportion, **The Nil Mind**, too, has all of its memory and information intact—just not active or visible on the surface, but one can access everything when needed.

The Nil Mind is the only means to touch the sacred space of **Nilness**. **Nilness** is not an entity or that which exists. To touch such a dimension that doesn't even exist, you must be nil of all the contents of the mind. End this book with the seriousness of finding out the truth for yourself by seeing reality as it is. No matter who you are, where you are from, what you do, what you didn't do, what you couldn't do, what you want to do, what you don't even know you need to do, no matter how unconsciously you are right now, no matter what you believe in, no matter what you are fearful and afraid about, no matter how old you are—if you have the yearning to find out for yourself what this life is all about and go at it head on without being distracted or influenced, unearthing the subtle qualities that you do have beneath all the facade of the mind—you will see that the answer to life is pretty simple. It is not as complicated as the mind projects it to be.

The Art of Nilness is not only the last chapter but is a part of all that is written and a way of being. Art is throwing light on the fundamental aspects of reality that are lost.

May you see the beauty of the mind, the oneness of existence, and the timeless reality.

THE END

~

Made in the USA
Monee, IL
03 July 2025

20421649R00133